Excel Formulas

140 Excel Formulas and Functions

with usage and examples

By Vijay Kumar

Introduction

Why should you learn Excel Formulas?

Thanks for downloading this book.

Excel is part of the Microsoft Office suite and the world's most widely used spreadsheet application used by Millions. Compared to other Spreadsheet programs Excel is very feature rich and popular and incorporated with so many built in Formulas and Functions. Even if you don't know the function name you can simply search the word you think related to a formula in the insert function box and you will get back the Formulas related to that word.

This book provides more than 140 Formulas and there use with examples for you to understand and use it in your day to day work.

Please keep in mind some of the new functions will not work in your Computer if you are using previous versions of Excel.

Things to remember while entering Formulas.

Formula can be entered in Excel by first entering the equal sign (=) followed by the formula name like this =SUM(A1:A100), opening and closing brackets are compulsory. Or else you can enter a plus sign and type the formula and the formula will be automatically converted to =+SUM(A2:A4). This is used for compatibility reason as when Excel was introduced the leading spreadsheet program was using the plus sign.

Relative, Absolute and Mixed reference

A reference means a cell (A1) or a range of cells (A1:A8) on a worksheet, and tells Excel where to look for the values or data you want to use in a formula.

Relative Reference

By default Excel follows relative reference. Say for example if you are adding two cells A1 and B1 in the cell C1 using the formula =SUM(A1+B1) and if you copy down the formula to C2 the Sum formula will automatically change the cell reference relatively to the next row to =SUM(A2+B2). If you copy the formula across the column to D1 the formula will change to SUM(B1+C1).

	A	B	C
1	1		
2	2	1	=A1
3		2	=A2

Absolute reference

Absolute reference means the cell reference will always refer to the same cell and for that you have to put a dollar sign before the column name and row number. As in the above example if you rewrite the formula to =SUM($A$1+$B$1) and if you copy down the formula the cell reference will not change relatively it will always get the sum of A1 and B1 wherever you paste the formula in the sheet.

By pressing the F4 key you can easily insert the dollar sign and if you keep on hitting the F4 key the reference will change to mixed and to relative.

	A	B	C
1	1		
2		1	=$A$1
3		1	=$A$1

Mixed reference

A mixed reference has either an absolute column and relative row, or absolute row and relative column in a formula. For example =$A1 will always refer to the A column, since there is no dollar sign before the row number if you copy across the formula the column name will not change but the row number will change.

Likewise if there is dollar sign before the row number (A$1) then the column number will change if you copy the formula but the row number will not change.

	A	B	C	D
1	1	2		
2		1	=A$1	
3			2	=B$1

Auto complete

You can use the auto complete feature of the Excel while entering the formula to speed up the Formula capturing. For example if you want to find the total of a range then you have to first enter the equal sign (=) followed by formula name SUM. While entering the formula if the formula name comes up as the first one in the auto complete list then you can press the TAB button and Excel will auto complete the formula with open brackets and after entering the arguments you can again press TAB button to automatically close the brackets.

Ctrl + Enter

If you want to enter formula to more than one cell then you can select the entire range and enter the formula, instead of pressing Enter you can press **Ctrl + Enter** to paste the formulas automatically to all the selected range.

CTRL + ` (grave accent)

If you got the worksheet and want to see all the formulas entered in the sheet you can press this shortcut **CTRL + `** key (just below the ESC key which has also the tilde (~) character). All the formula cells will expand to display the formula entered instead of the formula values.

Moving and Copying formulas

If you move (cut and paste) the formula from one cell to another then the formula will refer to the same cells. For example if you move =SUM(A1:B1) from the cell C1 to C8 it will still refer to the same cells.

If you copy the same formula from same C1 TO C8 then the formula will change to =SUM(A8:B8).

F9 to evaluate parts of a formula

Sometimes if you are using a nested formula like this =RIGHT(C22,LEN(C22)-FIND(" ",C22)) it will be very difficult to debug the formula if something goes wrong. In this case you can use the function key F9 to evaluate each nested formulas.

For example in this formula =SUM(A1:B1,D1:D3) if you select the first range A1:B1 and click F9 then you can see which all values are used and if you again press F9 then the values will get hardcoded to the formula.

Fill handle or using Fill series or Cntlr + D to fill the formula

Once you enter the formula you can use the Excel fill handle to fill down the formula. Once you completed entering the formula go back to the formula cell and put the mouse on the right hand down corner where a square dot is shown and the cursor will change to a black plus sign and you can double click the black plus sign and copy the entire formula down.

Keep in mind if there is any break in the data, means any rows are blank Excel will stop filling the formula just before that.

Also you can click on the Fill button > Down under Home tab to fill the formula down after selecting the cells you want to fill or you can use Fill button > Series and then select Autofill and click ok to copy the formula till there is a break in the data.

Or else you can use the shortcut Ctrl + D to fill down the formula. First you have to select the cell with the formula along with the other cells you want to copy down and press Ctrl + D to copy the formula down.

Using calculation operators in formulas

Operators specify the type of calculation that you want to perform on the elements of a formula. There is a default order in which calculations occur (this follows general mathematical rules), but you can change this order by using parentheses.

TYPES OF OPERATORS

There are four different types of calculation operators: Arithmetic, Comparison, Text concatenation, and Reference.

Arithmetic operators

+ (plus sign) is used for Addition, for examples like 10+15.
– (minus sign) is used for Subtraction, for examples 10-2.
Negation is used, for examples -6.
* (asterisk) is use for Multiplication, for examples 4*8.
/ (forward slash) is used for Division, for examples 25/9
% (percent sign) is used for Percent, for examples 25%
^ (caret) is use for Exponentiation, for examples 6^2.

Comparison operators

You can compare two values by using the operators given below and the result will always be a logical value TRUE or FALSE.

= (equal sign) meaning Equal to, For example A1 =C1.
> (greater than sign) meaning Greater than, For example A1>B1.
< (less than sign) meaning Less than, For example D1 <B1.
>= (greater than or equal to sign) meaning Greater than or equal to, For example A1>=B1.
<= (less than or equal to sign) meaning   Less than or equal to, For example A1<=B1.
<> (not equal to sign) meaning Not equal to, For example A1<>B1.

Text concatenation operator

Use the ampersand (&) to concatenate (join) one or more text strings to produce a single piece of text.

For example "East"&"west" will give you "Eastwest".

Reference operators

Combine ranges of cells for calculations with the following operators.

: (colon) is the Range operator, which produces one reference to all the cells between two references, including the two references A5:C15

, (comma) is the Union operator, which combines multiple references into one reference. For example SUM(A5:B15,G5:E15)

(space) Intersection operator, which produces one reference to cells common to the two references B7:D7 C6:C8.

EXCEL CALCULATION ORDER

In some cases, the order in which a calculation is performed can affect the return value of the formula, so it's important to understand how the order is determined and how you can change the order to obtain the results you want.

If you combine several operators in a single formula, Excel performs the operations in the order shown below. If a formula contains operators with the same precedence; say for example both multiplication and division operator, Excel evaluates the operators from left to right.

Operators

: (colon)
(single space)
, (comma)
− Negation (as in −3)
% Percent
^ Exponentiation
* and / Multiplication and division
+ and − Addition and subtraction
& Connects two strings of text (concatenation)
=
< >
<=
>=
<>

If you want to change the above order you can enclose that particular formula section in parentheses so that Excel will be forced to calculate whatever mentioned in the parentheses first.

For example if you enter this formula =5+4*6 you will get the answer 29 because first it will multiply and then it will add as per the operator precedence mentioned above. If you want to first add and then multiply then you can change the formula by adding the parentheses like this = (5+4) *6.

Common mistakes while capturing Formulas.

OPEN AND CLOSING PARENTHESES (BRACKETS)

In the formula whatever parentheses (brackets) you have opened should be closed. For example if you enter a SUM formula like this =SUM(A1:A6) you can see there is an opening and closing parentheses. If you nest the formula then there will be more opening and closing brackets for each formulas.

Excel automatically give separate color to each pairs of parentheses.

COLON TO INDICATE A RANGE

You should use the colon (:) for referring to a range like A1:A10. No other characters are allowed.

REQUIRED ARGUMENTS SHOULD BE ENTERED

All the required arguments in a formula should be entered and the arguments marked in square brackets can be avoided as per your requirement.

For example in this formula VLOOKUP(lookup_value, table_array, col_index-num, [range_lookup]) first three arguments or parameters has to be supplied and the last one range_lookup is optional which you can provide as per your requirement or you don't want to give.

NESTING OF FUNCTIONS

If you are nesting or clubbing together other functions as arguments then you can nest up to 64 levels of nested function in a formula, no more than that.

ENCLOSE OTHER SHEET NAMES IN SINGLE QUOTATION MARKS

If you refer to values or cells in another worksheet or workbook in a formula, and the name of that workbook or worksheet contains a non-alphabetical character, enclose the name within single quotation marks (').

INCLUDE THE PATH TO EXTERNAL WORKBOOKS

Make sure that each external reference you enter in a formula contains a workbook name and the path to the workbook.

ENTER NUMBERS WITHOUT FORMATTING

Make sure that you don't include the number formats while capturing numbers in a formula. If you put a dollar sign inside a formula before a cell reference the cell reference will change to absolute reference as dollar signs ($) are used to indicate absolute references.

DON'T ENCLOSE NUMBERS IN DOUBLE QUOTES

You should not enclose the numbers in double quotes when you supply the arguments to the formula. Only text arguments should be supplied in double quotes.

EXCEL FORMULAS NOT UPDATING AUTOMATICALLY

If the Excel formulas are not updating automatically then check whether the Formula calculation is set to manual under Formulas tab > Calculation options. If it is manual you can change the same to automatic.

How to force Excel Formulas to recalculate?

If for some reason, you need to have the Calculation option set to Manual, you can force the formulas to recalculate by clicking the Calculate button on the ribbon or by using one of the following shortcuts:

To recalculate the entire workbook:
Press F9, or
Click the Calculate Now button on the Formulas tab > Calculation group.

To recalculate an active sheet:
Press Shift + F9, or
Click Calculate Sheet on the Formulas tab.

To recalculate all sheets in all open workbooks:
Press Ctrl + Alt + F9.

And if you want to recheck dependent formulas and then recalculate all the formulas in all open workbooks.
Press CTRL+SHIFT+ALT+F9.

If you need to recalculate only one formula on a sheet, select the formula cell, enter the editing mode either by pressing F2 or double clicking the cell, and then press the Enter key.

Formula errors in Excel.

If Excel cannot properly evaluate a worksheet formula or function; it will display an error value such as #REF!, #NULL!, #DIV/0! - in the cell where the formula is located.

#NAME? Error

These are the some instances where this error will occur.

if you refer a formula that doesn't exist like instead of SUM you use SUMS
misspelled reference
text entered without enclosing double quotation marks
range defined without colon (:) this error will occur.

#REF! Error

Usually ilf you delete a cell or cell range which is used for calculating a formula this error will occur. Say if you are adding up the cells A1 and B1 and if you delete the B column this error will occur.

#DIV/0! ERROR

Divided by zero produces an infinity. EXCEL does this by producing #DIV/0! error.

#N/A ERROR

This error means not available, the data is not available. Given below is some instances where this error occurs.

While using the Lookup functions (HLOOKUP, LOOKUP, MATCH, or VLOOKUP) If the value you are searching is not there then this error will occur.
If any required arguments is omitted from a built-in or custom worksheet function this error will occur.

#NULL! ERROR

This type of error occurs usually occurs when two or more cell references are separated Incorrectly or unintentionally by a space in a formula. Like instead of coma =SUM(D1:D3 E1:E3) you have used space to separate these two ranges.

#NUM! ERROR

Generally #NUM! error occurs when your formula returns a value bigger than what excel can represent or wrong data type might be supplied in a function that requires a numeric argument.

#VALUE! ERROR

This error occurs when the variables specified to a function are of wrong types.

Or if you use the mathematical formula like SUM which take input as a number but chars or strings are being passed to it.

ERROR

This error occurs when your EXCEL column is not wide enough to accommodate a large value. For example, if a long number like 123123456456789789 is set to occupy a small cell then it would show up as #### error.

Widening the cell in can eradicate the error in above case but there are few more scenarios where this error can appear:

The result of your formula is too wide to fit in the cell.

If a negative number has been formatted to date or time then it will also produce this error. The reason being date and time are always supposed to be positive.

CIRCULAR REFERENCE ERROR

This error is rarest of all the errors to occur. This basically occurs when you define a result on a cell, which is also a part of one of your formula. For example if you add values from range A2 to A6 with its total at cell A7.

But what if I specify the result at cell A6 instead of A7. A6 being part of SUM range itself. Then we will get into circular references and this error might lead to wrong results.

The best way to overcome this to assign the results to a different cell and try to keep values and results as different as possible.

Debugging Formulas

If you want to debug the formula then you can use the Evaluate formula under the Formulas tab. Select the cell having the formula and click on Evaluate formulas for you to see the step by step calculation of the formula.

Also you can use the Trace Precedents and Trace Dependents under the Formula tab to find the precedent and dependent cells.

How to use This Book

Although I write this book with the intention to read this book cover to cover, you can read this book from middle or end, whatever way you want. Every Formula is self-explanatory so you can jump to any page you like.

For the ease of practicing I have made example files which you can download from my site **Exceltovba.com**. So before reading the book download the example file so that you can practice while you read.

My request to each readers is to go through all the example files so that you can learn very fast. The more you understand the examples the more experience you gain and the more you can implement the formulas in your day to day work.

Password is given at the end of this book.

Thanks again for downloading this book.

1. Compatibility

1.1 MODE

The MODE function returns the **most common value** or the most frequently occurring numbers in a group. For example, =MODE(1,2,2,3,3,3,3,34,4,5,5,5,6) returns 3.

Syntax:

=MODE (number1, [number2], ...)

Parameter list:

number1 – a number or cell reference that refers to numeric values.
number2 - [optional] a number or cell reference that refers to numeric values.

	A	B
1	Mode	=MODE (number1, [number2], ...)
2	3	=MODE(1,2,2,3,3,3,3,34,4,5,5,5,6)

Numbers can be supplied as numbers like the above example or ranges like =MODE(A1:A11,B4:B10) or named ranges, or cell references that contain numeric values. Up to 255 numbers can be supplied.

If the set of supplied numbers does not contain any duplicates, MODE will return #N/A error.

Points to note.

MODE is now classified as a "compatibility function". Microsoft recommends that MODE.SNGL or MODE.MULTI be used instead.

1.2. RANK

This function returns the rank, **the number indicating the rank from a list of numbers** in ascending or descending order. Use RANK when you want to provide a rank for items in a list, but you don't want to sort the list.

Syntax:

=RANK (number, ref, [order])

Parameter list:

number - the number whose rank you want to find.
ref - an array of, or a reference to, a list of numbers against you want to find the Rank. Nonnumeric values in ref are ignored.
order - [optional] whether to rank in ascending or descending order. Default order or if omitted it is 0 = descending order, 1 is ascending order.

Check the example file exceltovba.com-RANK.xls

	A	B	C	D	E	F
1	Name	Marks	Rank in Descending order	RANK(number,ref,[order])	Rank in Ascending order	RANK(number,ref,[order])
2	John	65	4	=RANK(B2,$B$2:$B$7,0)	3	=RANK(B2,$B$2:$B$7,1)
3	Jenu	85	1	=RANK(B3,$B$2:$B$7,0)	6	=RANK(B3,$B$2:$B$7,1)
4	Melvin	45	6	=RANK(B4,$B$2:$B$7,0)	1	=RANK(B4,$B$2:$B$7,1)
5	Rambo	66	3	=RANK(B5,$B$2:$B$7,0)	4	=RANK(B5,$B$2:$B$7,1)
6	Kevin	46	5	=RANK(B6,$B$2:$B$7,0)	2	=RANK(B6,$B$2:$B$7,1)
7	Roy	80	2	=RANK(B7,$B$2:$B$7,0)	5	=RANK(B7,$B$2:$B$7,1)

In this example Jenu has scored highest mark in the lot so he will get Rank 1 and Roy will get Rank 2 as he is the second highest followed by Rambo Rank 3 , John Rank 4, Kevin Rank 5 and Melvin Rank 6. It means the rank will be sorted in the Descending order (Column C) higher marks will have higher rank.

If you enter the third parameter 1 you can see the Rank will be sorted in reverse, in ascending order. It means Rank 1 will be Melvin as he has scored the lowest marks in the lot and Kevin Rank 2 followed by John, Rambo, Roy and Jenu.

Points to note.

This function has been replaced with new functions that provide improved accuracy and whose names better reflect their usage. The new functions are RANK.AVG and RANK.EQ (new version of RANK function).

As the name suggest RANK.AVG will provide you the rank and if more than one value has the same rank, the average rank is returned.

Although RANK function is still available for backward compatibility, you should consider using the new functions from now on, because this function may not be available in future versions of Excel.

2. Date and time

By default, Microsoft Excel for Windows uses the 1900 date system. Excel is storing the dates as serial numbers starting from 01/01/1900 means the first day of Jan 1900 is the day 1 and 2nd Jan 1900 is day 2 and January 1, 2008 is serial number 39448 because it is 39447 days after January 1, 1900. Microsoft Excel for the Macintosh uses the 1904 date system, so in Macintosh the date starts on January 1, 1904 so the serial number 1 means it is January 1, 1904.

If you want to see the serial number of any date just change the Number format of that cell to General format.

2.1. DATE

This function will create a **valid date from the values you supply** as Year, Month and Day. Return value will be serial number represents a particular date in Excel (if you change the date format to general you can see the serial number).

Syntax:

=DATE (year, month, day)

Parameter list:

year - the year to use when creating the date.
month - the month to use when creating the date.
day - the day to use when creating the date.

Check the example file exceltovba.com-DATE.xls

	A	B	C	D	E
1	Year	Month	Day	Date	DATE (year, month, day)
2	2015	5	5	05-05-15	=DATE(A2,B2,C2)
3	2016	6	4	04-06-16	=DATE(A3,B3,C3)
4	2013	7	10	10-07-13	=DATE(A4,B4,C4)
5	2012	8	31	31-08-12	=DATE(A5,B5,C5)
6	2011	9	15	15-09-11	=DATE(A6,B6,C6)
7	2010	10	19	19-10-10	=DATE(A7,B7,C7)

In this example you can see the date is been created in D column from the three parameters you supply as Year (A column), Month (B column) and Day (C column).

2.2. DATEVALUE

This function will **convert a date in text format to a valid date** and returns a serial number that represents a particular date in Excel.

Syntax:

=DATEVALUE (date_text)

Parameter list:

date_text - a valid date in text format. If date_text is a cell address, value of the cell must be text. If date_text is entered directly into the formula it must be enclosed in quotes.

Check the example file exceltovba.com-DATEVALUE.xlsx

	A	B	C
1	**Values**	**Results**	**DATEVALUE (date_text)**
2	12	42036	=DATEVALUE("01/02/2015")
3	4	41671	=DATEVALUE("01/02/2014")
4	1955	38384	=DATEVALUE("01/02/2005")
5		20191	=DATEVALUE(A2&"/"&A3&"/"&A4)

You can see in the last calculation we have used the & character to join all the dates as text in order to give the argument as text.

Excel is storing the dates as serial numbers starting from 01/01/1900 means the first day of Jan 1900 is the day one and 2nd Jan 1900 is day 2 like that. So if you want to get the serial number of a date entered as text you can use this function.

Points to note.

Will return a #VALUE error if date_text refers to a cell that does not contain a date formatted as text.

2.3. DAY

This function will **return the day as number (1 – 31)** from a Date and the return value will be any of the number from 1 to 31.

Syntax:

=DAY(serial_number)

Parameter list:

serial_number - a valid Excel date in serial number format.

Check the example file exceltovba.com-DATEVALUE.xlsx

	A	B	C
1	**Date**	**Results**	**DAY(date)**
2	25-12-56	25	=DAY(A2)
3	01-01-16	1	=DAY(A3)
4	28-09-13	28	=DAY(A4)

In this example only the Day part is been picked from the date.

2.4. DAYS

This function **returns the number of days between two dates**. This function is available from Excel 2013 and Excel for Mac 2011.

Syntax:

=DAYS(end_date, start_date)

Parameter list:

end_date - the end date.
start_date - the start date.

Check the example file exceltovba.com-DAYS.xlsx

	A	B	C	D
1	**Start Date**	**End Date**	**Results**	DAYS(end_date, start_date)
2	25-12-56	24-01-16	21579	=DAYS(B2,A2)
3	4566659875	24-01-16	#NUM!	=DAYS(B3,A3)
4	Hi	24-01-16	#VALUE!	=DAYS(B4,A4)
5		24-01-16	2	=DAYS(B5,"22/01/2016")

In this example we have calculated the number of days between two dates. You can see we are getting the #NUM value error when the range falls outside and #VALUE error when we try to compare the date and text.

Points to Note.

If either one of the date arguments is text, that argument will be treated as DATEVALUE(date_text) and returns an integer date.
If date arguments are numeric values that fall outside the range of valid dates, DAYS returns the #NUM! error value.
If date arguments are strings that cannot be treated as valid dates, DAYS returns the #VALUE! error value.
If you want to directly enter the dates like this =DAYS("22/05/2015","20/05/2015") then you must enclose the dates in quotation marks.

2.5. DAYS360

This function calculates the **number of days between two dates, based on a 360-day year** (twelve 30-day months) which is used in some accounting calculations. Use this function to help compute payments and receipts if your accounting system is based on twelve 30-day months.

Syntax:

=DAYS360 (start_date, end_date, [method])

Parameter list:

start_date - the start date. Dates should be entered by using the DATE function, or derived from the results of other formulas or functions.
end_date - the end date.
method - [optional] the type of day count basis to use. FALSE (default) or omitted is US method, TRUE is European method.

FALSE (default) or omitted - US method - If the starting date is the last day of a month, it becomes equal to the 30th day of the same month. When the end date is the last day of the month, and the start date is less than 30 days, the end date is set to the 1st of the next month, otherwise the end date is set to the 30th of the same month.
TRUE - European method. Starting dates and ending dates equal to the 31st of a month are set to the 30th of the same month.

Check the example file exceltovba.com-DAYS360.xlsx

	A	B	C	D	E
1	Start Date	End date	Results	DAYS360 (start_date, end_date, [method])	Explanation
2	24-01-15	24-01-16	360	=DAYS360(A2,B2)	30 days * 12 months
3	01-02-15	01-03-15	30	=DAYS360(A3,B3)	February calculates to 30 Days
4	31-01-15	01-02-15	1	=DAYS360(A4,B4)	Start date set to Jan 30
5	01-01-15	30-01-15	1	=DAYS360(B5,B7)	Number of days between 1/30/2015 and
6	01-01-15	31-12-15	360	=DAYS360(A6,B6)	Number of days between 1/1/2015 and 1
7	01-01-15	01-02-15	30	=DAYS360(A7,B7)	Number of days between 1/1/2015 and 2

2.6. EDATE

This function returns the **same date in future or past months** and returns the serial number of the date. Use EDATE to calculate maturity dates or due dates that fall on the same day of the month as the date of issue.

Syntax:

=EDATE (start_date, months)

Parameter list:

start_date - a date that represents the start date in a valid Excel serial number format.
months - the number of months before or after start_date. A positive value to get a future date and negative value for the past date.

	A	B	C	D	E
1	Date	Month	Results	Explanation	EDATE (start_date, months)
2	01-02-15	1	01-03-15	Date one months after	=EDATE(A2,B2)
3	01-02-15	-2	01-12-14	Date two months before	=EDATE(A3,B3)
4	01-02-15	6	01-08-15	Date six months after	=EDATE(A4,B4)
5	01-02-15	-4	01-10-14	Date four months before	=EDATE(A5,B5)
6	01-02-15	12	01-02-16	Date one year after	=EDATE(A6,B6)

Points to Note.

If start_date is not a valid date, EDATE returns the #VALUE! error value.
If month entered is not an integer it is truncated.

2.7. HOUR

This function will **return the hour as a number (0-23)** from a time and returns a number ranging from 0 (12.00 AM) to 23 (11:00 PM).

Syntax:

=HOUR (serial_number)

Parameter list:

serial_number - a valid time in a format Excel recognizes. Time may be entered as text strings within quotation marks (for example, "9:35 PM"), as decimal numbers (for example, 0.78125, which represents 6:45 PM), or as results of other formulas or functions (for example, TIMEVALUE("9:35 PM")).

Check the example file exceltovba.com-HOUR.xlsx

	A	B	C
1	Time	Result	HOUR (serial_number)
2	11:10 AM	11	=HOUR(A2)
3	31-01-16 11:10	11	=HOUR(A3)
4	1:25 PM	13	=HOUR(A4)
5	0.25	6	=HOUR(A4)
6	0.50	12	=HOUR(A4)
7	0.75	18	=HOUR(A4)
8		10	=HOUR("11.45")

Excel stores dates and times as serial numbers. For example, the date Jan 1, 2000 12:00 PM is equal to the serial number 32526.5 in Excel. To check that Excel is correctly recognizing a date or time, you can temporarily format the date as a number.

2.8. MINUTE

This function will get the **minute as a number (0-59)** from a time and returns a number between 0 and 59.

Syntax:

=MINUTE (serial_number)

Parameter list:

serial_number - a valid time in a format Excel recognizes.

Check the example file exceltovba.com-MINUTE.xls

	A	B	C
1	Time	Result	MINUTE (serial_number)
2	11:10 AM	10	=MINUTE(A2)
3	31-01-16 11:10	10	=MINUTE(A3)
4	1:25 PM	25	=MINUTE(A4)

Points to note.

Times can be supplied as text (e.g. "7:45 PM") or as decimal numbers (e.g. 0.5, which equals 12:00 PM).

Excel stores dates and times as serial numbers. For example, the date Jan 1, 2000 12:00 PM is equal to the serial number 32526.5 in Excel. To check that Excel is correctly recognizing a date or time, you can temporarily format the date as a number.

2.9. MONTH

This function will **procure the month as a number (1-12)** from a date and returns a number between 1 and 12.

Syntax:

=MONTH (date)

Parameter list:

date - a valid date in a format Excel recognizes.

Check the example file exceltovba.com-MONTH.xlsx

	A	B	C
1	Date	Result	MONTH (date)
2	27-01-15	1	=MONTH(A2)
3	06-Jul	7	=MONTH(A3)
4	Friday, December 23, 2011	12	=MONTH(A4)
5	13-Sep-10	9	=MONTH(A5)

In this example we have extracted month using MONTH function from various date formats.

2.10. NETWORKDAYS

This function returns a **number representing full working days between start_date and end_date**. Working days exclude weekends (by default Saturday and Sunday) and any dates you supply as holidays.

You can use this function to calculate the benefits of the employees that accumulate on the basis of number of days worked during a specific term.

Syntax:

=NETWORKDAYS (start_date, end_date, [holidays])

Parameter list:

start_date - the start date.
end_date - the end date.
holidays - [optional] a list of one or more dates that should be considered as holidays.

Check the example file exceltovba.com- NETWORKDAYS.xlsx

	A	B	C	D	E
1	Start Date	End Date	Result	=NETWORKDAYS (start_date, end_date, [holidays])	
2	01-01-16	15-01-16	11	=NETWORKDAYS(A2,B2)	Excluding the weekends
3	01-01-16	09-01-16	6	=NETWORKDAYS(A3,B3)	Excluding the weekends
4	01-01-16	31-01-16	21	=NETWORKDAYS(A4,B4)	Excluding the weekends
5	01-01-16	31-01-16	19	=NETWORKDAYS(A5,B5,B7:B8)	Excluding the weekends and the two holidays
6					
7	Holiday1	13-01-16			
8	Holiday2	20-01-16			

In this example for first three cases we are just calculating NETWORKDAYS without giving the third parameter so that it will eliminate only the weekends (by default Saturday and Sunday) and in the fourth case we are giving the two dates as holidays so this function will exclude these two holidays and the weekend in between these days.

If you want to make any other days as weekend then you should use the NETWORKDAYS.INTL function.

Points to note.

If any argument is not a valid date, NETWORKDAYS returns the #VALUE! error value.

2.11. NETWORKDAYS.INTL

This function will **calculate the working days between two dates excluding weekends** (by default Saturday and Sunday) and returns the number of days. This function is more versatile than the NETWORKDAYS function because it allows you to control which day or days of the week are considered weekends, you can make any of the day (like Monday or Tuesday) or any of the two days (like Tuesday and Wednesday or Wednesday and Thursday) as weekend.

Also you can specify holidays as fourth parameter so that holidays will not be counted along with weekend while calculating the number of days. This function was introduced in Excel 2010.

Syntax:

=NETWORKDAYS.INTL (start_date, end_date, [weekend], [holidays])

Parameter list:

start_date - the start date.
end_date - the end date.
weekend - [optional] setting for which days of the week should be considered weekends.
holidays - [optional] a reference to dates that should be considered non-work days.

Check the example file exceltovba.com- NETWORKDAYS.INTL.xlsx

	A	B	C	D	E
1	Start Date	End Date	Result	NETWORKDAYS.INTL (start_date, end_date, [weekend], [holidays])	
2	01-01-16	31-01-16	21	=NETWORKDAYS.INTL(A2,B2)	Excluding the weekends
3	01-01-16	31-01-16	22	=NETWORKDAYS.INTL(A3,B3,2)	Excluding the weekends (Sunday and Mon
4	01-01-16	31-01-16	23	=NETWORKDAYS.INTL(A4,B4,3)	Excluding the weekends (Monday, Tuesda
5	01-01-16	31-01-16	23	=NETWORKDAYS.INTL(A5,B5,4)	Excluding the weekends (Tuesday, Wedne
6	01-01-16	31-01-16	23	=NETWORKDAYS.INTL(A6,B6,5)	Excluding the weekends (Wednesday, Thu
7	01-01-16	31-01-16	22	=NETWORKDAYS.INTL(A7,B7,6)	Excluding the weekends (Thursday, Friday
8	01-01-16	31-01-16	21	=NETWORKDAYS.INTL(A8,B8,7)	Excluding the weekends (Friday, Saturday)
9	01-01-16	31-01-16	26	=NETWORKDAYS.INTL(A9,B9,11)	Excluding the weekends (Sunday only)
10	01-01-16	31-01-16	27	=NETWORKDAYS.INTL(A10,B10,12)	Excluding the weekends (Monday only)
11	01-01-16	31-01-16	27	=NETWORKDAYS.INTL(A11,B11,13)	Excluding the weekends (Tuesday only)
12	01-01-16	31-01-16	27	=NETWORKDAYS.INTL(A12,B12,14)	Excluding the weekends (Wednesday only
13	01-01-16	31-01-16	27	=NETWORKDAYS.INTL(A13,B13,15)	Excluding the weekends (Thursday only)
14	01-01-16	31-01-16	26	=NETWORKDAYS.INTL(A14,B14,16)	Excluding the weekends (Friday only)
15	01-01-16	31-01-16	26	=NETWORKDAYS.INTL(A15,B15,17)	Excluding the weekends (Saturday only)
16	01-01-16	31-01-16	19	=NETWORKDAYS.INTL(A16,B16,1,B18:B19)	Excluding the weekends (Sunday, Monday
17					
18	Holiday1	05-01-16			
19	Holiday2	12-01-16			

The weekend numbers (fourth parameter) are listed below.

Weekend number--------Weekend days

1 or omitted)--------------Saturday, Sunday
2------------------------------Sunday, Monday

```
3-------------------------------Monday, Tuesday
4-------------------------------Tuesday, Wednesday
5-------------------------------Wednesday, Thursday
6-------------------------------Thursday, Friday
7-------------------------------Friday, Saturday
11------------------------------Sunday only
12------------------------------Monday only
13------------------------------Tuesday only
14------------------------------Wednesday only
15------------------------------Thursday only
16------------------------------Friday only
17------------------------------Saturday only
```

Points to Note.

If start_date is greater than end_date, the function returns a negative value.

If start_date or end_date is out of range, NETWORKDAYS.INTL returns the #NUM! error.

If weekend is invalid, NETWORKDAYS.INTL returns the #VALUE! error.

2.12. NOW

This function will returns the serial number of the **current date and time**.

Syntax:

=NOW ()

NOW takes no parameters but requires empty parentheses. The value returned by NOW will continually update each time the worksheet is refreshed (for example, each time a value is entered or changed).

Use F9 to force the worksheet to recalculate and update the value.

Check the example file exceltovba.com- NOW.xls

	A	B	C
1	**Results**	NOW ()	
2	24-03-16 20:13	=NOW()	Todays date and time
3	17-03-16 20:13	=NOW()-7	Last weeks date and time
4	31-03-16 20:13	=NOW()+7	Next weeks date and time

In the above example you can see the first formula will return current date and time and the second formula will return last week's date and time if you put a -7 after the formula. Third formula will get next week's date and time if you put +7 after the formula.

Likewise you can add or subtract dates from Now funcion to get the dates you want.

2.13. SECOND

This function **returns the Second as a number (0-59)** from a Time and returns a number between 0 and 59.

Syntax:

=SECOND (serial_number)

Parameter list:

serial_number - a valid time in a format Excel recognizes.

Check the example file exceltovba.com- SECOND.xlsx

	A	B	C	D
1	Time	Result	SECOND (serial_number)	Explanation
2	27-01-16	0	=SECOND(B2)	Date format, No second
3	10:50:10 PM	10	=SECOND(B3)	10 seconds returned
4	8:17:39 PM	39	=SECOND(B4)	39 Seconds retuned

Times can be supplied as text (e.g. "7:45 PM") or as decimal numbers (e.g. 0.5, which equals 12:00 PM).

Excel stores dates and times as serial numbers. For example, the date Jan 1, 2000 12:00 PM is equal to the serial number 32526.5 in Excel. To check that Excel is correctly recognizing a date or time, you can temporarily format the date as a number.

2.14. TIME

This function **creates a time with hours, minutes, and seconds you provide** and returns a decimal number representing a particular time in Excel. Use it to create a valid time when you have (or can supply) these component values separately. Once you have a valid time, you can format it any way you like.

Syntax:

=TIME (hour, minute, second)

Parameter list:

hour - the hour for the time you wish to create.
minute - the minute for the time you wish to create.
second - the second for the time you wish to create.

Check the example file exceltovba.com- TIME.xlsx

	A	B	C	D	E	F
1	Hour	Minute	Second	Results	TIME (hour, minute, second)	Explanation
2	9	15	20	9:15:20 AM	=TIME(A2,B2,C2)	
3	10	30	0	10:30:00 AM	=TIME(A3,B3,C3)	
4	23	55	-1	11:54:59 PM	=TIME(A4,B4,C4)	Negative value adjusted
5	7	65	55	8:05:55 AM	=TIME(A5,B5,C5)	65 minuts adjusted to next hour

The decimal number returned by TIME is a value ranging from 0 (zero) to 0.99988426, representing the times from 0:00:00 (12:00:00 AM) to 23:59:59 (11:59:59 P.M.).

2.15. TIMEVALUE

This function returns the **decimal number of the time represented by a text string**. The decimal number is a value ranging from 0 (zero) to 0.99988426, representing the times from 0:00:00 (12:00:00 AM) to 23:59:59 (11:59:59 P.M.).

Syntax:

=TIMEVALUE (time_text)

Parameter list:

time_text - a text string that represents a time in any one of the Microsoft Excel time formats; for example, "6:45 PM" and "18:45" text strings within quotation marks that represent time.

Formula	Description	Result
=TIMEVALUE("8:24 AM")	Decimal part of a day, with only the time specified	0.35
=TIMEVALUE("22-Aug-2011 9:35 AM")	Decimal part of a day, with date and time specified	
	0.399305556	

2.16. TODAY

This function **returns the current date**. (a serial number representing the particular date in Excel).

Syntax:

=TODAY ()

This function has no parameters but requires empty parentheses. This function can be used to find out the age of a person in years like this. =YEAR(TODAY())-1980. This formula uses TODAY function as an argument in the YEAR function to get the current year and then subtract 1980 to get the difference in years.

= TODAY () function returns the current date.
= TODAY () +7 will return the current date plus 7 days.

2.17. WEEKDAY

This function **returns the day of the week as a number** between 1 (Sunday) and 7 (Saturday) by default. And if you want to change the Starting day from Sunday to Monday or any other day you can use the return type option.

Syntax:

=WEEKDAY (serial_number, [return_type])

Parameter list:

serial_number - the date for which you want to get the day of week.
return_type - [optional] a number 1-3 and 11-17 (return_type details given below) representing starting day of the week. Default is 1, Sunday (1st day) to Saturday (7th day).

return_type-----Number returned
1 or omitted-----Numbers 1 (Sunday) through 7 (Saturday)
2-------------------Numbers 1 (Monday) through 7 (Sunday)
3-------------------Numbers 0 (Monday) through 6 (Sunday)
11------------------Numbers 1 (Monday) through 7 (Sunday)
12------------------Numbers 1 (Tuesday) through 7 (Monday)
13------------------Numbers 1 (Wednesday) through 7 (Tuesday)
14------------------Numbers 1 (Thursday) through 7 (Wednesday)
15------------------Numbers 1 (Friday) through 7 (Thursday)
16------------------Numbers 1 (Saturday) through 7 (Friday)
17------------------Numbers 1 (Sunday) through 7 (Saturday)

Check the example file exceltovba.com- WEEKDAY.xlsx

	A	B	C	D
1	Date	Result	WEEKDAY (serial_number, [return_type])	
2	01-03-16	3	=WEEKDAY(A2)	Numbers 1 (Sunday) through 7 (Saturday)
3	01-03-16	2	=WEEKDAY(A3,2)	Numbers 1 (Monday) through 7 (Sunday)
4	29-02-16	0	=WEEKDAY(A4,3)	Numbers 0 (Monday) through 6 (Sunday)
5	01-03-16	2	=WEEKDAY(A5,11)	Numbers 1 (Monday) through 7 (Sunday)
6	01-03-16	1	=WEEKDAY(A6,12)	Numbers 1 (Tuesday) through 7 (Monday)
7	01-03-16	7	=WEEKDAY(A7,13)	Numbers 1 (Wednesday) through 7 (Tuesday)
8	01-03-16	6	=WEEKDAY(A8,14)	Numbers 1 (Thursday) through 7 (Wednesday)
9	01-03-16	5	=WEEKDAY(A9,15)	Numbers 1 (Friday) through 7 (Thursday)
10	01-03-16	4	=WEEKDAY(A10,16)	Numbers 1 (Saturday) through 7 (Friday)
11	01-03-16	3	=WEEKDAY(A11,17)	Numbers 1 (Sunday) through 7 (Saturday)

In this example you can see the all the options will give a day number from 1 to 7 except if you use the return_type 3 which starts the day on 0 (Monday) and ends on 6 (Sunday).

2.18. WEEKNUM

This function returns the **week number** for a given date and returns a number between 1 and 54.

There are two systems for this function:

System 1 - week containing January 1 as the first week of the year, and is numbered week 1.

System 2 - week containing the first Thursday of the year as the first week of the year, and is numbered as week 1 (commonly known as the European week numbering system).

Syntax:

=WEEKNUM (serial_num, [return_type])

Parameter list:

serial_num - a valid Excel date in serial number format.
return_type - [optional] the day the week begins. Default is 1.

```
return_type----Week begins on---System
1 or omitted----Sunday------------------1
2-------------------Monday----------------1
11-----------------Monday----------------1
12-----------------Tuesday----------------1
13-----------------Wednesday------------1
14------------------Thursday--------------1
15-----------------Friday-------------------1
16-----------------Saturday----------------1
17-----------------Sunday------------------1
21-----------------Monday-----------------2
```

Check the example file exceltovba.com- WEEKNUM.xlsx

	A	B	C	D
1	Date	Result	WEEKNUM (serial_num, [return_type])	Week begins on
2	01-01-16	1	=WEEKNUM(A2)	Sunday
3	01-01-16	1	=WEEKNUM(A3,2)	Monday
4	01-01-16	1	=WEEKNUM(A4,11)	Monday
5	01-01-16	1	=WEEKNUM(A5,12)	Tuesday
6	01-01-16	1	=WEEKNUM(A6,13)	Wednesday
7	01-01-16	1	=WEEKNUM(A7,14)	Thursday
8	01-01-16	1	=WEEKNUM(A8,15)	Friday
9	01-01-16	1	=WEEKNUM(A9,16)	Saturday
10	01-01-16	1	=WEEKNUM(A10,17)	Sunday
11	01-01-16	53	=WEEKNUM(A11,21)	Monday

In this example you can see the all the options are using the System 1 except the last one which is using the System 2 in which the week containing the first Thursday of the year is the first week of the year. So in this case 01 Jan 2016 is Friday so it will not be counted as the first week, 04th Jan 2016 will be the first week as it has the first Thursday of the year.

2.19. WORKDAY

This function returns a **date according to the number of working days you specify before or after a date** (the starting date). Use a positive number for days to calculate future dates, and a negative number for past dates. By default, WORKDAY will exclude weekends (Saturday and Sunday).

For example =WORKDAY("01/01/2016",3) will give you the result 42375 which is the serial number of the date 06-01-16. 1st Jan is Friday, 4th Jan is Monday and 5th Jan is Tuesday, since you have given the second parameter as 3 you will get the fourth workday date as answer which is 06 Jan 2016.

Syntax:

=WORKDAY (start_date, days, [holidays])

Parameter list:

start_date - the date from which to start.
days - The working days before or after start_date.
holidays - [optional] A list dates that should be considered non-work days.

Check the example file exceltovba.com- WORKDAY.xlsx

	A	B	C	D	E
1	Start Date	Days	Result	WORKDAY (start_date, days, [holidays])	
2	01-01-16	5	08-01-16	=WORKDAY(A2,B2)	Excluding the weekends
3	01-01-16	-1	31-12-15	=WORKDAY(A3,B3)	Excluding the weekends
4	01-01-16	10	15-01-16	=WORKDAY(A4,B4)	Excluding the weekends
5	01-01-16	10	19-01-16	=WORKDAY(A5,B5,B7:B8)	Excluding the weekends and the two holidays
6					
7	Holiday1	08-01-16			
8	Holiday2	05-01-16			

In this example for the first three we are only calculating the days in the past and present without giving the third parameter holidays and in the last one we have given two dates (third parameter) as holidays to exclude from the calculation of the future Workday date.

In some countries the Weekends will differ. In that case you must use the WORKDAY.INTL function as this function can set the weekend to Friday and Saturday or Monday or Sunday or any day or any two consecutive days of your choice.

2.20. WORKDAY.INTL

This function returns **a date in working days in future or past from the start date and no. of days you provide**. This function is same like WORKDAY function and the only difference is you can set the weekend to Friday and Saturday or Monday or Sunday or any day or any two consecutive days of your choice

By default, WORKDAY.INTL will exclude weekends (Saturday and Sunday). WORKDAY.INTL can also optionally take into account holidays (fourth parameter). For the Holiday's argument, supply a range that contains holiday date or dates which will be treated as non-working days and will not be included in the result.

Syntax:

=WORKDAY.INTL (start_date, days, [weekend], [holidays])

Parameter list:

start_date - the start date.
days - the end date.
weekend - [optional] setting for which days of the week should be considered weekends (weekend number given below).
holidays - [optional] a list of one or more dates that should be considered non-work days.

weekend-number--------Weekend days

1 or omitted---------------Saturday, Sunday
2--------------------------Sunday, Monday
3--------------------------Monday, Tuesday
4--------------------------Tuesday, Wednesday
5--------------------------Wednesday, Thursday
6--------------------------Thursday, Friday
7--------------------------Friday, Saturday
11-------------------------Sunday only
12-------------------------Monday only
13-------------------------Tuesday only
14-------------------------Wednesday only
15-------------------------Thursday only
16-------------------------Friday only
17-------------------------Saturday only

Check the example file exceltovba.com- WORKDAY.INTLxlsx

	A	B	C	D	E
1	Start Date	Days	Result	WORKDAY.INTL (start_date, days, [weekend], holidays)	
2	01-01-16	5	08-01-16	=WORKDAY.INTL(A2,B2,1)	Weekend Saturday, Sunday
3	01-01-16	5	08-01-16	=WORKDAY.INTL(A3,B3,2)	Weekend Sunday, Monday
4	01-01-16	5	08-01-16	=WORKDAY.INTL(A4,B4,3)	Weekend Monday, Tuesday
5	01-01-16	5	08-01-16	=WORKDAY.INTL(A5,B5,4)	Weekend Tuesday, Wednesday
6	01-01-16	5	08-01-16	=WORKDAY.INTL(A6,B6,5)	Weekend Wednesday, Thursday
7	01-01-16	5	06-01-16	=WORKDAY.INTL(A7,B7,6)	Weekend Thursday, Friday
8	01-01-16	5	07-01-16	=WORKDAY.INTL(A8,B8,7)	Weekend Friday, Saturday
9	01-01-16	-5	26-12-15	=WORKDAY.INTL(A9,B9,11)	Weekend Sunday only
10	01-01-16	5	07-01-16	=WORKDAY.INTL(A10,B10,12)	Weekend Monday only
11	01-01-16	5	07-01-16	=WORKDAY.INTL(A11,B11,13)	Weekend Tuesday only
12	01-01-16	5	07-01-16	=WORKDAY.INTL(A12,B12,14)	Weekend Wednesday only
13	01-01-16	5	06-01-16	=WORKDAY.INTL(A13,B13,15)	Weekend Thursday only
14	01-01-16	5	06-01-16	=WORKDAY.INTL(A14,B14,16)	Weekend Friday only
15	01-01-16	10	15-01-16	=WORKDAY.INTL(A15,B15,17,B17:B18)	Excluding the weekend (Saturday, Holiday1, H
16					
17	Holiday1	08-01-16			
18	Holiday2	05-01-16			

In this example in the last calculation we have supplied two holiday dates as fourth parameter to exclude these dates along with the weekend Saturday.

Points to note.

If start_date or start_date + day or holiday is invalid, WORKDAY.INTL returns the #NUM! error.
If weekend is invalid, WORKDAY.INTL returns the #VALUE! error.

2.21. YEAR

This function **returns the year from a date**. For example =YEAR(01-01-00) will return 1900 and =YEAR(20-03-15) will return 2015.

Syntax:

=YEAR (date)

Parameter list:

date - a date from which to extract the year.

Excel only handles dates after 1/1/1900 so you can use this function from the dates starting from 1900.

3. Engineering

3.1. CONVERT

The CONVERT function converts a number in **one measurement system to another**. For example, you can use CONVERT to convert feet into meters, pounds into kilograms, gallons into liters, and for many other unit conversions.

Syntax:

=CONVERT (number, from_unit, to_unit)

Parameter list:

number - the numeric value to convert.
from_unit - the unit to convert.
to_unit – to the unit you want to convert.

Check the example file exceltovba.com-CONVERT.xlsx

	A	B	C
1	Result	CONVERT (number, from_unit, to_unit)	Description
2	0.90718474	=CONVERT(2, "lbm", "kg")	Converts 2 pound mass to kilograms
3	37	=CONVERT(98.6, "F", "C")	Converts 98.6 degrees Fahrenheit to Celsius
4	#N/A	=CONVERT(2.5, "ft", "sec")	Data types are not same, error is returned

Shown below are the various units that are available to the CONVERT function. In all cases, Unit can be used for either from_unit or to_unit, it should me mentioned in quotation marks.

Weight and mass---------------------From_unit or to_unit

Gram--"g"
Slug---"sg"
Pound mass (avoirdupois) -----------"lbm"
U (atomic mass unit) --------------------"u"
Ounce mass (avoirdupois) -------------"ozm"
Grain--"grain"
U.S. (short) hundredweight-------------"cwt" or "shweight"
Imperial hundredweight-----------------"uk_cwt" or "lcwt" ("hweight")
Stone---------------------------------------"stone"
Ton--"ton"
Imperial ton--------------------------------"uk_ton" or "LTON" ("brton")

Distance------------------------From_unit or to_unit
Meter-----------------------------------"m"
Statute mile----------------------------"mi"
Nautical mile--------------------------"Nmi"
Inch-------------------------------------"in"

Foot-------------------------------------"ft"
Yard-------------------------------------"yd"
Angstrom--------------------------------"ang"
Ell---------------------------------------"ell"
Light-year-------------------------------"ly"
Parsec----------------------------------"parsec" or "pc"
Pica (1/72 inch)--------------------------"Picapt" or "Pica"
Pica (1/6 inch)--------------------------"pica"
U.S survey mile (statute mile)--------"survey_mi"

Time   From_unit or to_unit
Year   "yr"
Day   "day" or "d"
Hour   "hr"
Minute "mn" or "min"
Second "sec" or "s"

Pressure   From_unit or to_unit
Pascal   "Pa" (or "p")
Atmosphere   "atm" (or "at")
mm of Mercury "mmHg"
PSI   "psi"
Torr   "Torr"

Force   From_unit or to_unit
Newton"N"
Dyne   "dyn" (or "dy")
Pound force   "lbf"
Pond   "pond"

Energy-------------------------From_unit or to_unit
Joule-------------------------------------"J"
Erg---------------------------------------"e"
Thermodynamic calorie ----------------"c"
IT calorie--------------------------------"cal"
Electron volt-----------------------------"eV" (or "ev")
Horsepower-hour------------------------"HPh" (or "hh")
Watt-hour--------------------------------"Wh" (or "wh")
Foot-pound------------------------------"flb"
BTU--------------------------------------"BTU" (or "btu")

Power--------------------------------From_unit or to_unit
Horsepower------------------------"HP" (or "h")
Pferdestärke------------------------"PS"

Watt--------------------------------"W" (or "w")

Magnetism------From_unit or to_unit
Tesla----------------------"T"
Gauss---------------------"ga"

Temperature-------------From_unit or to_unit
Degree Celsius------------"C" (or "cel")
Degree Fahrenheit-------"F" (or "fah")
Kelvin-----------------------"K" (or "kel")
Degrees Rankine----------"Rank"
Degrees Réaumur---------"Reau"

Volume (or l iquid measure)----From_unit or to_unit
Teaspoon---------------------------------------"tsp"
Modern teaspoon----------------------------"tspm"
Tablespoon-------------------------------------"tbs"
Fluid ounce-------------------------------------"oz"
Cup--"cup"
U.S. pint---"pt" (or "us_pt")
U.K. pint--"uk_pt"
Quart--"qt"
Imperial quart (U.K.)---------------------------"uk_qt"
Gallon---"gal"
Imperial gallon (U.K.) ------------------------"uk_gal"
Liter--"l" or "L" ("lt")
Cublc angstrom --------------------------------"ang3" or "ang^3"
U.S. oil barrel----------------------------------"barrel"
U.S. bushel-------------------------------------"bushel"
Cublc feet--------------------------------------"ft3" or "ft^3"
Cubic inch--------------------------------------"in3" or "in^3"
Cubic light-year -------------------------------"ly3" or "ly^3"
Cubic meter------------------------------------"m3" or "m^3"
Cubic Mile--------------------------------------"mi3" or "mi^3"
Cubic yard--------------------------------------"yd3" or "yd^3"
Cubic nautical mile----------------------------"Nmi3" or "Nmi^3"
Cubic Pica--------------------------------------"Picapt3", "Picapt^3", "Pica3" or "Pica^3"
Gross Registered Ton-------------------------"GRT" ("regton")
Measurement ton (freight ton) ------------------"MTON"

Area   From_unit or to_unit
International acre------------------------"uk_acre"
U.S. survey/statute acre----------------"us_acre"
Square angstrom-------------------------"ang2" or "ang^2"

Are---"ar"
Square feet------------------------------------"ft2" or "ft^2"
Hectare---------------------------------------"ha"
Square inches----------------------------------"in2" or "in^2"
Square light-year------------------------------"ly2" or "ly^2"
Square meters --------------------------------"m2" or "m^2"
Morgen--"Morgen"
Square miles-----------------------------------"mi2" or "mi^2"
Square nautical miles--------------------------"Nmi2" or "Nmi^2"
Square Pica------------------------------------"Picapt2", "Pica2", "Pica^2" or "Picapt^2"
Square yards-----------------------------------"yd2" or "yd^2"

Information----------From_unit or to_unit
Bit----------------------------"bit"
Byte--------------------------"byte"

Speed-------------------From_unit or to_unit
Admiralty knot- -------------"admkn"
Knot----------------------------"kn"
Meters per hour-------------"m/h" or "m/hr"
Meters per second----------"m/s" or "m/sec"
Miles per hour -------------"mph"

Points to note.

If the input data types are incorrect, CONVERT returns the #VALUE! error value.
If the unit does not exist, CONVERT returns the #N/A error value.
If the unit does not support a binary prefix, CONVERT returns the #N/A error value.
If the units are in different groups, CONVERT returns the #N/A error value.
Unit names and prefixes are case-sensitive.

4. Financial

4.1. FV

This function **calculates the future value of an investment** assuming periodic constant payments with a constant interest rate.

Syntax:

=FV (rate, nper, pmt, [pv], [type])

Parameter list:

rate - the interest rate per period.
nper - the total number of payment periods.
pmt - the payment made each period. Must be entered as a negative number as the money is going out.
pv - [optional] the present value of future payments. If omitted, assumed to be zero. Must be entered as a negative number.
type - [optional] when payments are due. 0 = end of period, 1 = beginning of period. Default is 0.

Check the example file exceltovba.com-FV.xlsx

	A	B	C
1	Description	Data	
2	Annual interest rate	8%	
3	Number of payments	12	
4	Amount of the payment	-300	
5	Present value	-500	
6		FV (rate, nper, pmt, [pv], [type])	
7	Future value of an investment with present value (due at the beginning of the period)	$4,301.38	=FV(B2/12, B3, B4, B5, 1)
8	Future value without considering the present value (due at the end of the preiod)	$3,734.98	=FV(B2/12,B3,B4)
9	Future value without considering the present value (due at the beginning of the preiod)	$3,759.88	=FV(B2/12,B3,B4,,1)

In this example we are calculating the Future value of an investment. First we are calculating the future value considering the present value invested and also the payment is been done at the beginning of the year.

Second one we are calculating the future value without any initial investment and the payment due with the end of the period.

And third we are calculating the future value without any initial investment and the payment is due at the beginning of the period.

Points to note.

1. Units for rate and nper must be consistent. For example, if you make monthly payments on a five-year loan at 10 percent annual interest, use 10%/12 (annual rate/12 = monthly interest rate) for rate and 5*12 (60 payments total) for nper. If you make annual payments on the same loan, use 10% (annual interest) for rate and 5 (5 payments total) for nper.

2. If pmt is for cash out (i.e deposits to saving, etc), payment value must be negative; for cash received (income, dividends), payment value must be positive.

4.2. PMT

This function **calculates the periodic payment for a loan** based on constant payment and constant interest rate. For example if you are buying a Car worth $20000 with 24 months loan repayment and 7 percent interest you can calculate the monthly payment and how much principal and interest you are paying each month.

Syntax:

=PMT (rate, pmt, pv, [fv], [type])

Parameter list:

rate - the interest rate for the loan, if you are paying monthly you have to divide by 12.
pmt - the total number of payments for the loan (12 months of 36 months).
pv - the present value, or total value of all loan payments now.
fv - [optional] the future value, or a cash balance you want after the last payment is made. Defaults to 0 (zero).
type - [optional] when payments are due. 0 = end of period. 1 = beginning of period. Default is 0.

Example 1: Calculating the Car Loan repayment amount.

Check the example file exceltovba.com-PMT.xlsx Sheet1

	A	B	C
1	Car Value	-10000	Negative value to indicate money is leaving the bank.
2	Interest rate	8%	Annual rate, for monthly rate we are dividing by 12.
3	Period in months	48	12 months x 4 Years
4			PMT (rate, pmt, pv, [fv], [type])
5	Monthly Payment	$244.13	=PMT(B2/12,B3,B1)
6			
7	Total paid	$11,718.20	Period * Monthly payment
8	Interest paid	$1,718.20	Total paid - Car value

In this example file we are calculating how much we will pay as principal and interest for the car loan for a period of 48 months. Car value is $10000 and we are procuring a loan at 8 percent for a term of 48 months. Formula for this is =PMT(B2/12,B3,B1).

First parameter we will enter the interest rate since we are paying monthly we will divide the interest rate by 12 , 8%/12 to get the monthly interest rate.

Second we are entering the period in months here it is 48.

Third parameter we are entering the Car value or principal amount or loan taken, we have put a negative sign to indicate the amount is been debited from our bank.

After entering the formula you will get the monthly amount to be paid for this loan for 48 months.

You can now multiply the Period with the Monthly payments to get the total loan amount paid which is $11,718.20 and if you subtract this from the Principal you will get the interest paid for this loan which is $1,718.20.

Points to Note.

The payment returned by PMT includes principal and interest but will not include any taxes, fees, hidden charges, reserve payments or fees.

Make sure that the first and second parameters you supply should be correct. For example if you are calculating a monthly payment of a loan for 4 years @ 10%, then 10%/12 will be the rate and 4 * 12 will be nper. If you make annual payment for the same loan then 10% will be the rate and 4 will be nper.

If it is quarterly, rate will be 10%/4 and 16 will be the nper (4 years multiplied by 4 quarter).

There may be slight difference in the amount calculated in Excel 2007 and Excel 2010 as algorithm used is different in both and Excel 2010 calculation is more accurate.

Example 2: Calculating the amount to be saved monthly to get 75000 at the end of 10 Years.

Check the example file exceltovba.com-PMT.xlsx Sheet2

	A	B	C
1	Details	Data	
2	Amount to save	$75,000	
3	Interest rate annualy	9%	
4	No. of years	10	
5			PMT (rate, pmt, pv, [fv], [type])
6	Amount to save monthly for 10 Years	($387.57)	=PMT(B3/12,B4*12,0,B2)

Here the goal is to build a corpus of 75000 at the end of 10 years. So in the formula first parameter we are entering the interest rate as monthly, second parameter we are entering the term for 10 years which is 10 years * 12 months which is 120, third parameter we are entering 0 because the present value is 0 from which we want to build it to 75000 and the last parameter we are supplying the amount we should build which is 75000.

4.3. IPMT

This function **returns the interest payment** for an investment for a given period with a constant payment and interest rate.

Syntax:

IPMT(rate, per, nper, pv, [fv], [type])

Parameter list:

Rate – the interest rate per period.
Per - the period for which you want to find the interest and must be in the range 1 to nper.
nper - the total number of payment periods in an annuity.
Pv - the present value, or the lump-sum amount that a series of future payments is worth right now.
Fv - the future value, or a cash balance you want to attain after the last payment is made. If fv is omitted, it is assumed to be 0 (the future value of a loan, for example, is 0).
Type - the number 0 or 1 and indicates when payments are due. If type is omitted, it is assumed to be 0. 0 = at the end of the period, 1 = at the beginning of the period.

Check the example file exceltovba.com-IPMT.xlsx

	A	B	C
1	Details	Data	
2	Loan amount	8000	
3	Annual Interest rate	10%	
4	Period in years	3	
5			
6	Interest for the month	1	
7	Interest for the month	2	
8			IPMT(rate, per, nper, pv, [fv], [type])
9	Interest for first month	($66.67)	=IPMT(B3/12,B6,B4*12,B2)
10	Interest for second month	($65.07)	=IPMT(B3/12,B7,B4*12,B2)
11	Interest due in the last year if payments are made yearly.	($292.45)	=IPMT(B3,3,3,B2)

In this example we are calculating the interest amount for first month in the cell B9 using the formula =IPMT(B3/12,B6,B4*12,B2). Since we are paying monthly we are calculating the monthly rate by dividing it by 12, second parameter we are supplying the month number, first month, from the total term of 36 months.Third parameter we are providing the total period by multiplying the month with years to arrive at 36 and the fourth parameter is the loan amount itself.

Like that the second month is calculated in the cell B10.

And in cell B11 we are calculating the interest due in the last year (3rd year), here we are considering the interest rate annually so no need to divide by 12 and **per** and **Nper** are same because we are finding the interest for the last year which is 3 so **per** will be 3 and **Nper** is 3 because we are paying only three times in the loan period.

Points to Note.

Make sure that the first and second parameters you supply should be correct. For example if you are calculating a monthly payment of a loan for 4 years @ 10%, then 10%/12 will be the rate and 4 * 12 will be nper. If you make annual payment for the same loan then 10% will be the rate and 4 will be nper.

If it is quarterly, rate will be 10%/4 and 16 will be the nper (4 years multiplied by 4 quarter).

4.4. PV

This function **calculates the present value of a loan** or investment based on constant interest rate.

Syntax:

=PV (rate, nper, pmt, [fv], [type])

Parameter list:

rate - the interest rate per period. If it is 10% annual rate and makes monthly payment then it is 10%/12.
nper - total number of payment periods. If it is a two year loan then 2 * 12, 24 periods.
pmt - the payment made for each period. If pmt is omitted, you must include the fv argument.
fv – [Optional] the cash balance you want to attain after the last payment is made. If fv is omitted cash payment will be 0 at the end of the loan. If fv is omitted, you must include the pmt argument.
type - [Optional]. when will be payment due, 0 or omitted = end of the period and 1 = beginning of the period

Check the example file exceltovba.com-PV.xlsx

	A	B	C
1	Payment amount	-1200	Negative value to indicate money is leaving the bank.
2	Interest rate	8%	Annual rate, for monthly rate we are dividing by 12.
3	Period in months	48	12 months x 4 Years
4			PV (rate, nper, pmt, [fv], [type])
5	Loan amount	$49,154.30	=PV(B2/12,B3,B1)

In this example we are calculating the Loan amount. Payment amount is the monthly payment amount including principal and interest (-negative sign to indicate the cash is leaving your bank), interest rate is 8% which we are dividing by 12 to get the monthly interest rate and period is 48 (12 months x 4).

If you are paying quarterly, rate will be 8%/4 and 16 (4 period x 4 years) will be the nper.

4.5. NPER

This function **returns the number of periods for an investment** based on constant periodic payments and interest rate.

Syntax:

=NPER (rate, pmt, pv, [fv], [type])

Parameter list:

rate - the interest rate per period.

pmt - the payment made each period.

pv - the present value, or total value of all payments now.

fv - [optional] the future value, or a cash balance you want after the last payment is made. Defaults is 0.

type - [optional] when payments are due. 0 = end of period. 1 = beginning of period. Default is 0.

Check the example file exceltovba.com-NPER.xlsx

	A	B	C
1	Description	Data	
2	Annual interest rate	12%	
3	Payment made each period	-100	
4	Present value of investment	-1000	
5	Future value of Investment	10000	
6			
7	Periods for the investment (payment made at the beginning of the period)	59.67	=NPER(B2/12, B3, B4, B5, 1)
8	Periods for the investment (payments are made at the end of the period)	60.08	=NPER(B2/12, B3, B4, B5)

In this example we are finding out the period by investing at the beginning of the period and at the end of the period.

By entering 1 as fifth parameter will calculate the payment at the beginning of the period and the present value of investment is shown as negative because cash have been flown out.

Points to note.

Interest rate is 8% which we are dividing by 12 to get the monthly interest rate and period is 48 (12 months x 4). If you are paying quarterly, rate will be 8%/4 and 16 (4 period x 4 years) will be the nper.

PMT normally includes principal and interest but not taxes, reserve payments, fees or any other charges.

4.6. RATE

This function will **return the interest rate per period** of an annuity

Syntax:

=RATE (nper, pmt, pv, [fv], [type], [guess])

Parameter list:

nper - the total number of payment periods.

pmt - the payment made each period and will not be changed.

pv - the present value, or total value of all loan payments now.

fv - [optional] the future value, or a cash balance you want after the last payment is made. Defaults to 0 (zero).

type - [optional] when payments are due. 0 = end of period. 1 = beginning of period. Default is 0.

guess - [optional] your guess on the rate. Default is 10%.

Check the example file exceltovba.com-RATE.xlsx

	A	B	C
1	Description	Data	
2	Total Loan years	5	
3	Monthly payment	-300	
4	Amount of the loan	10000	
5			
6	RATE (nper, pmt, pv, [fv], [type], [guess])		
7	Monthly rate of the loan	2%	=RATE(B2*12, B3, B4)
8	Annual rate of the loan	26.10%	=RATE(B2*12,B3,B4)*12

In this example file we are first finding out the monthly rate and then converting to annual rate by multiplying with 12.

Points to note.

RATE is calculated by iteration. If the results of RATE do not converge within 0.0000001 after 20 iterations, RATE returns the #NUM! error value.

You must be consistent with units for guess and nper. If you make monthly payments on a five-year loan at 8 percent annual interest, use 8%/12 for guess and 5*12 for nper. If you make annual payments on the same loan, use 8% for guess and 5 for nper.

5. Information

5.1. CELL

This function will provide the **information about a cell** and returns a text value. Use CELL to extract a wide range of information about reference by supplying the info_type you supply.

Syntax:

=CELL (info_type, [reference])

Parameter list:

info_type - the type of information to return about the reference, info_type is given below.
reference - [optional] The reference from which to extract information.

Points to note.

Always wrap the info_type in double quotes. For the formula: =CELL("col", C19) will return 3. See below for a full list of info_types and a key to the codes that CELL returns when the info_type is format.

When reference refers to more than one cell, CELL will return information about the first cell in reference.

If you already applied the Info_type argument in the CELL function as "format" and you later apply a different format to the referenced cell, you must recalculate the worksheet to update the results of the CELL function

The following info types can be used with the CELL function:

info_type	Description
"address"	Reference of the first cell in reference, as text.
"col"	Column number of the cell in reference.
"color"	The value 1 if the cell is formatted in color for negative values; otherwise returns 0 (zero).
"contents"	Value of the upper-left cell in reference; not a formula.
"filename"	Filename (including full path) of the file that contains reference, as text. Returns empty text ("") if the worksheet that contains reference has not yet been saved.
"format"	Text value corresponding to the number format of the cell. The text values for the various formats are shown in the following table. Returns "-" at the end of the text value if the cell is formatted in color for negative values. Returns "()" at the end of the text value if the cell is formatted with parentheses for positive or all values.
"parentheses"	The value 1 if the cell is formatted with parentheses for positive or all values; otherwise returns 0.

"prefix"	Text value corresponding to the "label prefix" of the cell. Returns single quotation mark (') if the cell contains left-aligned text, double quotation mark (") if the cell contains right-aligned text, caret (^) if the cell contains centered text, backslash (\) if the cell contains fill-aligned text, and empty text ("") if the cell contains anything else.
"protect"	The value 0 if the cell is not locked; otherwise returns 1 if the cell is locked.
"row"	Row number of the cell in reference.
"type"	Text value corresponding to the type of data in the cell. Returns "b" for blank if the cell is empty, "l" for label if the cell contains a text constant, and "v" for value if the cell contains anything else.
"width"	Column width of the cell, rounded off to an integer. Each unit of column width is equal to the width of one character in the default font size.

If you are using the Info_type argument as "format" then you will get the cell format of the cell your are referring to as per the details given below. For example if the cell format is General you will get G and if it is number you will get F2.

If the Excel format is		The CELL function returns
General	"G"	
0		"F0"
#,##0		",0"
0		"F2"
#,##0.00		",2"
$#,##0_);($#,##0)		"C0"
$#,##0_);[Red]($#,##0)		"C0-"
$#,##0.00_);($#,##0.00)	"C2"	
$#,##0.00_);[Red]($#,##0.00)		"C2-"
0%		"P0"
0.00%		"P2"
0.00E+00		"S2"
# ?/? or # ??/??		"G"
m/d/yy or m/d/yy h:mm or mm/dd/yy	"D4"	
d-mmm-yy or dd-mmm-yy		"D1"
d-mmm or dd-mmm		"D2"
mmm-yy		"D3"
mm/dd		"D5"
h:mm AM/PM		"D7"
h:mm:ss AM/PM		"D6"
h:mm		"D9"
h:mm:ss		"D8"

Check the example file exceltovba.com-CELL.xlsx

	A	B
1	**Values**	
2	75	
3	Good Morning	
4	65.36	
5	25.78	
6		
7	**Results**	**CELL (info_type, [reference])**
8	6	=CELL("col",E20)
9	24	=CELL("row", A25)
10	Good Morning	=CELL("contents", A3)
11	v	=CELL("type", A2)
12	G	=CELL("format",A4)
13	F2	=CELL("format",A5)

In this example first we are calculating the column number of the cell E20 using CELL functions first parameter "col". Second we are calculating the row number of the cell A25 using "row" as the first parameter.

Third we are using the "contents" as the first parameter to find the contents of the cell A3 which is "Good Morning". Fourth we are finding the type of the cell content using the "type" as the first parameter which is the data type value which is v.

Fifth and Sixth we are using the first parameter as "format" to find out the format of the cell contents mentioned in the second parameter. Fifth we are getting 'G' because the cell content of A4 is General format so we will get the answer G. Likewise the content of A5 is formatted as number so we will get the answer as F2.

5.2. INFO

This function returns the information about the **current operating environment**.

Syntax:

=INFO(type_text)

Parameter list:

type_text - text that specifies what type of information you want returned.

Points to Note.

Below are the Type_text you can use and the corresponding details you will get when you use the type_text.

Type_text	Returns
"directory"	Path of the current directory or folder.

"numfile"	Number of active worksheets in the open workbooks.		

"origin"   Returns the absolute cell reference of the top and leftmost cell visible in the window, based on the current scrolling position, as text prepended with "$A:". The actual value returned depends on the current reference style setting. Using D9 as an example, the return value would be:

A1 reference style   "$A:$D$9".

R1C1 reference style   "$A:R9C4"

"osversion"   Current operating system version, as text.

"recalc"   Current recalculation mode; returns "Automatic" or "Manual".

"release"   Version of Microsoft Excel, as text.

"system"   Name of the operating environment:
Macintosh = "mac"
Windows = "pcdos"

Examples:

=INFO("numfile")   Will return number of active worksheets.
=INFO("recalc")   Will return recalculation mode for the workbook.

5.3. ISBLANK

This function **tests if a cell is empty** and returns a logical value (TRUE or FALSE). For example, =ISBLANK(A1) will return TRUE if A1 is empty, and FALSE if A1 contains text or formulas. Sometimes the cell looks empty but may not be the case be.

Syntax:

=ISBLANK (value)

Parameter list:

value - the value to check.

Check the example file exceltovba.com-ISBLANK.xlsx

	A	B	C
1	Value	Result	ISBLANK (value)
2	25	FALSE	=ISBLANK(A2)
3		FALSE	=ISBLANK(A3)
4		TRUE	=ISBLANK(A4)
5	2450	FALSE	=ISBLANK(A5)
6		FALSE	=ISBLANK(A6)

In this example fourth row returns TRUE as A4 cell is actually empty. A2 and A5 has values in it and returns FALSE and A3 and A6 returns false because A3 has a single quote and A6 has a single space which is not visible when you see the Excel sheet.

5.4. ISERR

This function **checks for any error value except #N/A** and returns a logical value TRUE or FALSE.

Syntax:

=ISERR (value)

Parameter list:

value - the value to check for any error but #N/A.

Check the example file exceltovba.com-ISERR.xlsx

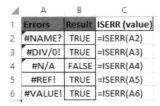

	A	B	C
1	**Errors**	**Result**	**ISERR (value)**
2	#NAME?	TRUE	=ISERR(A2)
3	#DIV/0!	TRUE	=ISERR(A3)
4	#N/A	FALSE	=ISERR(A4)
5	#REF!	TRUE	=ISERR(A5)
6	#VALUE!	TRUE	=ISERR(A6)

In the Example you can see except #N/A error rest of the errors we are getting the result as True.

Points to note.

Use the ISERR function to see if a cell has an error except for #N/A. This includes #VALUE!, #REF!, #DIV/0!, #NUM!, #NAME?, or #NULL!. Normally the value is supplied as a cell address so that you can club and use this with other function.

5.5. ISERROR

This function **checks for any error value (#N/A, #VALUE!, #REF!, #DIV/0!, #NUM!, #NAME?, or #NULL!)** and returns a logical value TRUE or FALSE.

Syntax:

=ISERROR (value)

Parameter list:

value - the value to check for any error.

5.6 ISEVEN

This function is used to check whether the **numeric value is an even number** and returns TRUE if the number is even or else will return FALSE. If value is not numeric, ISEVEN will return the #VALUE error.

=ISEVEN (value)

Usually, value is supplied as a cell address like this =ISEVEN (A1)

=ISEVEN(2) will return TRUE.
=ISEVER(1) will return FALSE.

5.7. ISFORMULA

This function **returns TRUE if a cell contains a formula** or else it will return FALSE. For example =ISFORMULA(A1) will return TRUE if the A1 cell has any formula like =SUM(A4:A5) or =A4+A5.This function is introduced in Excel 2013.

Syntax:

ISFORMULA(reference)

Parameter list:

reference - reference to the cell you want to test, can be a cell reference, a formula, or a name that refers to a cell.

5.8. ISLOGICAL

This function checks if a **value is logical (TRUE or FALSE)** and return a logical value (TRUE or FALSE).

Syntax:

=ISLOGICAL (value)

Parameter list:

value - the value to test as logical.

Points to note.

1 and 0 (zero) are not evaluated as TRUE and FALSE.

5.9. ISNA

This function will **test for the #N/A error** and returns TRUE when value is #N/A and FALSE if not.

Syntax:

=ISNA (value)

Parameter list:

value - the value to check if #N/A.

Normally value is supplied as a cell address like this =ISNA(B2).

5.10. ISNONTEXT

This function **tests for a non-text value** and returns a logical value TRUE or FALSE. ISNONTEXT will return TRUE when value is a non-text value and FALSE if not. ISNONTEXT will also return TRUE for blank cells.

Syntax:

=ISNONTEXT (value)

Parameter list:

value - the value to check.

Often, value is supplied as a cell address.

5.11. ISNUMBER

This function will **return TRUE if value is a number** and FALSE if not. For example, =ISNUMBER(A1) will return TRUE if A1 contains a number or a formula that returns a numeric value. If A1 contains text, ISNUMBER will return FALSE.

Syntax:

=ISNUMBER (value)

Parameter list:

value - the value to check.

Check the example file exceltovba.com-ISNUMBER.xlsx

	A	B	C	D
1	**Value**	**Result**		
2	25	TRUE	=ISNUMBER(A2)	
3	HI	FALSE	=ISNUMBER(A3)	
4		FALSE	=ISNUMBER(A4)	
5	16-03-15	TRUE	=ISNUMBER(A5)	
6	#N/A	FALSE	=ISNUMBER(A6)	

In the same example file open the second Sheet2, in that we are first checking whether any number is entered in the cell C8 using ISNUMBER and if number is entered then IF function will call the first VLOOKUP formula to search using the Employee number and if the name is entered then IF function will call second VLOOKUP to search by name..

Formula used =IF(ISNUMBER(C8),**VLOOKUP(C8,$A$2:$C$6,3,0)**,VLOOKUP(C8,$B$2:$C$6,2,0))

	A	B	C	D	E	F	G
1	**Emp No.**	**Name**	**Bonus**				
2	25	Melvin	$1,000.00				
3	99	Joy	$2,500.00				
4	106	Mary	$2,750.00				
5	75	Vijay	$1,500.00				
6	55	Roger	$ 900.00				
7							
8	**Type Emp no. or Name**		Joy				
9	**Bonus given**		$2,500.00				
10	=IF(ISNUMBER(C8),VLOOKUP(C8,$A$2:$C$6,3,0),VLOOKUP(C8,$B$2:$C$6,2,0))						

5.12. ISODD

This function **tests if a value is odd** and returns TRUE when a numeric value is odd and FALSE when a numeric value is even. For example, =ISODD(A1) will return TRUE if A1 contains the number 7 and FALSE if A1 contains the number 6.

Usually the value is supplied as a cell address.

Syntax:

=ISODD (number)

Parameter list:

number - the numeric value to test and if number is not an integer it is truncated.

Check the example file exceltovba.com-ISODD.xlsx

	A	B	C
1	**Values**	**Result**	**ISODD (number)**
2	2	FALSE	=ISODD(A2)
3	3	TRUE	=ISODD(A3)
4	4	FALSE	=ISODD(A4)
5	5	TRUE	=ISODD(A5)
6	6	FALSE	=ISODD(A6)
7	7	TRUE	=ISODD(A7)
8	8	FALSE	=ISODD(A8)
9	9	TRUE	=ISODD(A9)

5.13. ISREF

This function **checks the value is a reference**. ISREF will return TRUE when value is a reference and FALSE if not.

Syntax:

=ISREF (value)

Parameter list:

value - The value to check.

For example, =ISREF(A1) will return TRUE and =ISREF("apple") will return false.

5.14. ISTEXT

This function **checks if the value is text**. ISTEXT will return TRUE when value is text or else it will return FALSE.

Syntax:

=ISTEXT (value)

Parameter list:

value - the value to check.

For example, =ISTEXT(A1) will return TRUE if A1 contains "James". Often, value is supplied as a cell address.

5.15. N

This function **converts a value to a number**.

Syntax:

=N (value)

Parameter list:

value - the value to convert to a number.

Values will be converted as given below when using this function.

A number will return that number itself.
A date, in one of the built-in date formats available in Microsoft Excel will return the serial number of that date
If the value is TRUE it will return 1.
If the value is FALSE it will return 0.
If it is an error value, such as #DIV/0! It will return the error value itself.
And anything else this function will return 0.

In most cases it unnecessary to use the N function as Excel automatically converts values as necessary. This function is provided for compatibility with other spreadsheet programs.

There is a tricky use of N() that allows you to use it as a way to leave in-cell comments. The technique is to add a plus sign at the end of your formula with a comment as text in quotes inside the N() function like this:

=SUM(A1:A10) + N("This one adds the cells from A1 to A10")

When you click on that cell, you'll see both the formula and the comment in the formula bar. The N() function has no impact on the result of the function. In fact, you can add more than one N() function to a formula to annotate other functions, constants, or both.

5.16. NA

This function **creates a #N/A error**. In other words Use NA to generate the #N/A. #N/A means "not available" or "no value available". For example, you can use NA to flag cells that are empty or missing information

Syntax:

=NA ()

Points to note.

NA takes no arguments, but you must provide empty parentheses.

5.17. TYPE

This function **returns a numeric code representing the type of value in a cell**. Use TYPE when the behavlor of another function depends on the type of value In a particular cell.

Syntax:

=TYPE (value)

Parameter list:

value - the value to check the type of.

If the value is Number TYPE returns 1.
If the value is Text TYPE returns 2.
If the value is Logical value TYPE returns 4.
If the value Is Error value TYPE returns 16.
If the value is Array TYPE returns 64.

Points to note.

TYPE is most useful when you are using functions that can accept different types of data, such as ARGUMENT and INPUT. Use TYPE to find out what type of data is returned by a function or formula.

You cannot use TYPE to determine whether a cell contains a formula. TYPE only determines the type of the resulting, or displayed, value. If value is a cell reference to a cell that contains a formula, TYPE returns the type of the formula's resulting value.

6. Logical

6.1. AND

This function **tests multiple conditions** and returns TRUE if all arguments evaluate to TRUE else it will return FALSE.

Syntax:

=AND (logical1, [logical2], ...)

Parameter list:

logical1 - the first condition or logical value to evaluate.
logical2 - [optional] the second condition or logical value to evaluate. Up to a maximum of 255 conditions.

Points to note.

The arguments must evaluate to logical values, such as TRUE or FALSE, or the arguments must be arrays or references that contain logical values.

If an array or reference argument contains text or empty cells, those values are ignored.
If the specified range contains no logical values, the AND function returns the #VALUE! error value.

Please go through the examples given below.

=AND(TRUE, TRUE) will return TRUE because all the arguments are TRUE.
=AND(TRUE, FALSE) will return FALSE because one of the argument is FALSE.
=AND(2+4=6, 4+5=9) will return TRUE because both the cases are true 2 + 4 is 6 and 4 + 5 is 9.

It can be useful to extend the functionality of functions like IF.

=IF(AND(A1>0,A1<5), "Approved", "Denied")

This formula will return "Approved" only if the value in A1 is greater than 0 and less than 5.

In the below example we are calculating how many of the students have scored 50 marks (passing mark) or more in all subjects, we will get TRUE if all the students have scored 50 or above.

Check exceltovba.com-AND.xlsx

	A	B	C	D	E	F
1	Name	Maths	English	Physics	Passed	Formula used
2	Jenu	54	66	88	TRUE	=AND(B2>'=$C$13,C2>'=$C$13,D2>'=$C$13)
3	Melvin	13	96	49	FALSE	=AND(B3>'=$C$13,C3>'=$C$13,D3>'=$C$13)
4	Vijay	69	74	88	TRUE	=AND(B4>'=$C$13,C4>'=$C$13,D4>'=$C$13)
5	Maya	56	42	35	FALSE	=AND(B5>'=$C$13,C5>'=$C$13,D5>'=$C$13)
6	Roger	10	90	60	FALSE	=AND(B6>'=$C$13,C6>'=$C$13,D6>'=$C$13)
7	Williams	66	28	21	FALSE	=AND(B7>'=$C$13,C7>'=$C$13,D7>'=$C$13)
8	John	24	Absent	80	FALSE	=AND(B8>'=$C$13,C8>'=$C$13,D8>'=$C$13)
9	Ray	86	36	97	FALSE	=AND(B9>'=$C$13,C9>'=$C$13,D9>'=$C$13)
10	Jennifer	75	76	45	FALSE	=AND(B10>'=$C$13,C10>'=$C$13,D10>'=$C$13)
11	Hary	72	63	76	TRUE	=AND(B11>'=$C$13,C11>'=$C$13,D11>'=$C$13)
12						
13	Pass mark		50			

6.2. IF

This function will **test for a specific condition** and returns the value your supply if a condition is true and another value if it's false.

Syntax:

=IF (logical_test, [value_if_true], [value_if_false])

Parameter list:

logical_test - a value or logical expression that can be evaluated as TRUE or FALSE.
value_If_true - the value to return when logical_test evaluates to TRUE.
value_If_false - [optional] The value to return when logical_test evaluates to FALSE.

When you are constructing a test with IF, you can use any of the following logical operators:

Comparison operator	Meaning	Example
=	equal to	A1=D1
>	greater than	A1>D1
>=	greater than or equal to	A1>=D1
<	less than	A1<D1
<=	less than or equal to	A1<=D1
<>	not equal to	A1<>D1

Please go through the examples given below to further illustrate the use of IF.

Example 1.

Check exceltovba.com-IF.xlsx.

D4

	A	B	C	D	E
1	Name	Sales	Target	Result	Commission
2	John	1500	5000	Not Achieved	75
3	Roy	2500	1500	Achieved	250
4	Jessy	3500	4000	Not Achieved	175
5	Donald	1300	1100	Achieved	130
6	Luiz	2900	2500	Achieved	290
7	Arnold	3300	3000	Achieved	330
8					

Here we are checking whether the Sales target of each employee has met and if the particular employee has achieved the Target, Company will be give ten percent of the Sales as commission or else will provide five percent.

So in the Results Column we are using the formula =IF(B2>=C2,"Achieved","Not Achieved") to find out whether the employees has achieved the Target and in the commission column we are calculating the commission using the formula =IF(B2>=C2,B2*10%,B2*5%). Instead of hardcoding the percentages 10 and 5 you can enter the value as cell reference so that if the commission rate changes you have to just change two cell values only.

Example 2.

Check exceltovba.com-IF-2.xlsx

H6

	A	B	C	D	E
1	Product	Special Offer	Order Value	Discount	Amount to pay
2	Cement	No	$ 3,000.00	$ -	$ 3,000.00
3	Glass	Yes	$ 2,000.00	$ 200.00	$ 1,800.00
4	Wood	Yes	$ 800.00	$ -	$ 800.00
5	Mixing Agent	No	$ 500.00	$ -	$ 500.00
6	Iron Rod	Yes	$ 2,500.00	$ 250.00	$ 2,250.00
7	Bricks	No	$ 2,000.00	$ -	$ 2,000.00

Here we are checking whether there is special offer for the product and the order value crosses thousand dollars. If these two conditions are met then we will provide a discount of 10 percent. So in the discount column we are calculating the discount amount using the formula =IF(AND(B2="Yes",C2>=1000),C2*10%,0).

Here we are first checking whether the word Yes is written in the Special offer column and the Order value is greater than 1000 using the AND function. If these two conditions are met then IF formula will calculate the ten percent discount or else it will return 0 to the discount column.

Once that is done we will deduct the discount from Order value to reach the final amount to pay.

6.3. IFERROR

This function **returns a value you specify** if a formula evaluates to an error; otherwise, returns the result of the formula. Use the IFERROR function to trap and handle errors in a formula.

Syntax:

=IFERROR (value, value_if_error)

Parameter list:

value - the value, reference, or formula to check for an error.
value_if_error - the value to return if the formula evaluates to an error. The following error types are evaluated: #N/A, #VALUE!, #REF!, #DIV/0!, #NUM!, #NAME?, or #NULL!.

Points to note.

If Value or Value_if_error is an empty cell, IFERROR treats it as an empty string value ("").
If Value is an array formula, IFERROR returns an array of results for each cell in the range specified in value.

This function is very useful, if you comparing two excel sheets using Vlookup formula and you will get #N/A error if the value is not there in other Excel sheet. Suppose you are doing some calculations based on the result like multiplying the values then it will result in another #N/A error. So to avoid you can put the VLOOKUP formula inside IFERROR like this =IFERROR(VLOOKUP(A1,table,2,FALSE),0) to get 0 if there is an error.

Or else we can return the text like this Not found. You can write the formula like this
=IFERROR(VLOOKUP(A1,table,2,FALSE),"Not Found")

6.4. NOT

This function **reverses the value of it arguments** and returns a reversed logical value. In other words if any of the formulas evaluates to TRUE and If you use this function you will get FALSE and you will get TRUE if the formula evaluates to FALSE.

Syntax:

=NOT (logical)

Parameter list:

logical - a value or logical expression that can be evaluated as TRUE or FALSE.

Examples given below.

=NOT(FALSE) will give you the answer TRUE as it reversed the logical value.
=NOT(4+4=8) will give you the value FALSE because sum of 4+4 is 8 and is true and it reverses the logical value to FALSE.
=NOT(4+3=8) will give you the value TRUE because sum of 4+3 is not 8 and is false and so it reverses the logical value to TRUE.

Why would you want to use this function? A common example is to reverse the behavior of another function. For example, If the cell A1 is blank, then the formula =ISBLANK(B1) will return TRUE.

NOT can be used to reverse this result to FALSE like this:

=NOT(ISBLANK(A1))

In essence, by adding NOT, you are able to create a formula that behaves like ISNOTBLANK, which doesn't exist in Excel.

6.5. OR

This function **tests multiple conditions** with OR and returns TRUE if any of the arguments is correct and FALSE if not. Up to 255 conditions you can check.

Syntax:

=OR (logical1, [logical2], ...)

Parameter list:

logical1 - The first condition or logical value to evaluate.
logical2 - [optional] the second condition or logical value to evaluate.

Points to note.

The arguments must evaluate to logical values such as TRUE or FALSE, or in arrays or references that contain logical values.

If an array or reference argument contains text or empty cells, those values are ignored.
If the specified range contains no logical values, OR returns the #VALUE! error value.
You can use an OR array formula to see if a value occurs in an array. To enter an array formula, press CTRL+SHIFT+ENTER.

Examples:

=OR(TRUE) will get the answer as true because one argument is TRUE.
=OR(2+2=1,2+8=5) will get the answer as FALSE as both the arguments are wrong, 2+2 is not 1 and 2+8 is not 5.
=OR(TRUE,FALSE,TRUE) will get TRUE one of the argument is TRUE

=IF(OR(3+1=1,2+9=5,5+15=20),"Correct","Not Correct") will get the answer Correct as one of the arguments is true. In this case you are nesting it with another function IF so that you can define your own words as answer In this case Correct or if you want to get an answer as YES then Instead of Correct use the word YES.

=IF(OR(A1>75,B1<75), "Pass", "Fail") will get Pass if the value in A1 is greater than 75 or the value in B1 is lesser than 75 or else we will get the answer Fail.

In the below example we are calculating the processing charges for the payment we have received as Cash or Cheque. If it is Cash or Cheque we will charge Rs.10. So in this case we are clubbing the function IF to get the results.

Check exceltovba.com-OR.xlsx

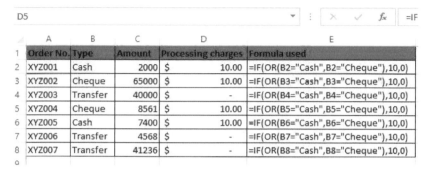

	A	B	C	D	E
1	Order No.	Type	Amount	Processing charges	Formula used
2	XYZ001	Cash	2000	$ 10.00	=IF(OR(B2="Cash",B2="Cheque"),10,0)
3	XYZ002	Cheque	65000	$ 10.00	=IF(OR(B3="Cash",B3="Cheque"),10,0)
4	XYZ003	Transfer	40000	$ -	=IF(OR(B4="Cash",B4="Cheque"),10,0)
5	XYZ004	Cheque	8561	$ 10.00	=IF(OR(B5="Cash",B5="Cheque"),10,0)
6	XYZ005	Cash	7400	$ 10.00	=IF(OR(B6="Cash",B6="Cheque"),10,0)
7	XYZ006	Transfer	4568	$ -	=IF(OR(B7="Cash",B7="Cheque"),10,0)
8	XYZ007	Transfer	41236	$ -	=IF(OR(B8="Cash",B8="Cheque"),10,0)

In the below example we are calculating the processing charges for the payment we have received as Cash or Cheque. If it is Cash or Cheque will charge Rs.10 as processing charge and if it is a transfer there won't be any charge. So in this case we are clubbing this function with IF to get the results.

6.6. FALSE

This function **generates the logical value FALSE.**

Syntax:

=FALSE ()

The FALSE function takes no arguments. Use FALSE to generate the logical value FALSE. For example, to return FALSE if the value in A1 < 0, use the formula:

=IF(A1<0, FALSE())

Note that you can also just use enter the word FALSE directly into a cell or formula and Excel will interpret this as the logical value FALSE. For example, these formulas are functionally identical:

=IF(A1<0, FALSE())
=IF(A1<0, FALSE)

The FALSE function is provided primarily for compatibility with other spreadsheet programs.

6.7. TRUE

This function **generates the logical value TRUE.**

Syntax:

=TRUE ()

The TRUE function takes no arguments.

Microsoft has provided TRUE function for compatibility with other spreadsheet applications and there is no need to use it in almost all cases.

If you want to enter TRUE, or provide TRUE as a result in a formula, you can just use enter the word TRUE directly into a cell or formula and Excel will interpret this as the logical value TRUE. For example, these formulas are functionally identical:

=IF(A1<0, TRUE())
=IF(A1<0, TRUE)

Also note that logical expressions themselves will automatically generate TRUE and FALSE results. For example if the cell B7 has the value 110 then =B7>90 will return the logical value TRUE.

6.8. IFNA

This function returns the value you specify if the formula returns #N/A; error otherwise, returns the result of the formula. This function was introduced in Excel 2013.

Syntax:

IFNA(value, value_if_na)

Parameter list:

Value - the formula that is checked for the #N/A error value.
Value_if_na - the value to return if the formula evaluates to the #N/A error value.

Points to note.

If Value or Value_if_na is an empty cell, IFNA treats it as an empty string value ("").
If Value is an array formula, IFNA returns an array of results for each cell in the range specified in value.

For example in this formula =IFNA(VLOOKUP("Joy",$A$5:$B$10,0),"Not found") if the name Joy is not there in the lookup table it will return #N/A error and IFNA function will return Not Found which you have specified at the end of the formula .

7. Lookup and reference

7.1. ADDRESS

This function **creates a cell address from a given row and column**. For example, ADDRESS(5,3) returns $C$5. As another example, ADDRESS(250,53) returns $BA$250. You can use other functions, such as the ROW and COLUMN functions, to provide the row and column number arguments for the ADDRESS function.

Syntax:

=ADDRESS (row_num, col_num, [abs_num], [a1], [sheet_text])

Parameter list:

row_num - the row number to use in the cell address.
col_num - the column number to use in the cell address.
abs_num - [optional] the address type (i.e. absolute, relative). Defaults to absolute.
a1 - [optional] the reference style, A1 vs R1C1. Default is A1 style.
sheet_text - [optional] the name of the worksheet to use. Defaults to current sheet.

Abs_num key:

1 or omitted	Absolute
2	Absolute row; relative column
3	Relative row; absolute column
4	Relative

a1 – This is optional

A logical value that specifies the A1 or R1C1 reference style. In A1 style, columns are labeled alphabetically, and rows are labeled numerically. In R1C1 reference style, both columns and rows are labeled numerically. If the A1 argument is TRUE or omitted, the ADDRESS function returns an A1-style reference; if FALSE, the ADDRESS function returns an R1C1-style reference.

sheet_text - This is Optional.

A text value that specifies the name of the worksheet to be used as the external reference. For example, the formula =ADDRESS(1,1,,,"Sheet2") returns Sheet2!$A$1. If the sheet_text argument is omitted, no sheet name is used, and the address returned by the function refers to a cell on the current sheet.

Examples:

=ADDRESS(5,3) returns $C$5
=ADDRESS(5,3,2) returns C$5 , Absolute row and Relative column.
=ADDRESS(5,3,2,FALSE) returns R5C[3] absolute row; relative column in R1C1 reference style

7.2. AREAS

This function **returns the number of areas in a reference**.

Syntax:

=AREAS (reference)

Parameter list:

reference - a reference to a cell or range of cells.

Usage notes:

Reference can include more than one reference. You must separate multiple references with a comma and wrap them in an extra set of parentheses. Otherwise, Excel will think the commas indicate multiple parameters and generate an error.

Examples:

=AREAS((E17:E19,K16:K18,M8)) will return 3 as there are three references.
=AREAS(B2:D4) will return 1 as there is only one reference.

7.3. CHOOSE

This function will **return a value from a list based on index number you specify**. For example if there are three values and you specify the index number as 1 it will return the first value and if you specify 2 it will return the second value.

Syntax:

=CHOOSE (index_num, value1, [value2], ...)

Parameter list:

index_num - the value to choose. A number between 1 and 254.
value1 - the first value from which to choose.
value2 - [optional] the second value from which to choose.

Points to note.

If index_num is less than 1 or greater than the number of the last value in the list, CHOOSE returns the #VALUE! error value.
If index_num is a fraction, it is truncated to the lowest integer before being used.
If index_num is an array, every value is evaluated when CHOOSE is evaluated.

The value arguments to CHOOSE can be range references as well as single values.

For example, the formula =SUM(CHOOSE(2,A1:A10,B1:B10,C1:C10)) will first evaluate the CHOOSE function to return =SUM(B1:B10) the second range based on the index number you have specified, in this case 2.

7.4. COLUMN

This function will **return the column number** of a reference.

Syntax:

=COLUMN ([reference])

Parameter list:

reference - [optional] reference to a cell or range of cells.

Points to note.

Reference can be a single cell address or a range of cells.
Reference is optional and will default to the cell in which the COLUMN function exists.
Reference cannot include multiple references or addresses.

Examples:

=COLUMN() will return the column number in which this formula is entered. If you have entered in A1 you will get column number as 1.

=COLUMN(B1:Z1) will return the column number as 2 as the cell range starts from second column. Other columns will not be considered.

7.5. COLUMNS

This function will **return the number of columns** in an array or reference. For example, the formula =COLUMNS(A1:E1) returns the number 5 as there are five columns from A to E.

Syntax:

=COLUMNS (array)

Parameter list:

array - A reference to a range of cells.

Points to note.

Array can be an array, an array formula, or a reference to a single contiguous group of cells.

Examples:

=COLUMNS(B1:Z1) will return 25 as there are 25 columns from B to Z.

=COLUMNS({1,2,3,4;5,6,7,8}) will return the column number as 4. There are two 4-column rows, containing 1,2,3 and 4 in the first row and 5, 6,7 and 8 in the second row.

7.6. HLOOKUP

This function **searches for a value in the first row of a table**. At the match column, it retrieves a value from the specified row. Use HLOOKUP when lookup values are located in the first row of a table. This function is same like VLOOKUP, whereas VLOOKUP searches vertically, HLOOKUP searches horizontally.

This function will look up a value in a table by matching on the first row.

Syntax:

=HLOOKUP(lookup_value, table_array, row_index_num, [range_lookup])

Parameter list:

lookup_value - the value to look up.
table_array - the table from which to retrieve data.
row_index_num - the row number from which to retrieve data.
range_lookup - [optional] a boolean to indicate exact match or approximate match. Default is TRUE = approximate match, FALSE = exact match.

Points to note.

Range_lookup controls whether value needs to match exactly or not. The default is TRUE = allow non-exact match.

Set range_lookup to FALSE to require an exact match and values in the first row of table do not need to be sorted.

If range_lookup is TRUE (the default setting), a non-exact match will cause the HLOOKUP function to match or match the nearest value in the table that is still less than value.

If range_lookup is TRUE (the default setting) make sure that lookup values in the first row of the table are sorted in ascending order. Otherwise, HLOOKUP may return an incorrect or unexpected value.

If there are more than one value in the table you are looking this function will pick the first value only.

Check the example HLOOKUP.XLSX Sheet1

	A	B	C	D	E	F
1	Name	John	Arnold	Jomy	Melvin	
2	Marks in Physics	54	58	84	83	
3	Marks in Maths	65	73	92	80	
4	Marks in Chemistry	51	95	93	55	
5						
6	HLOOKUP (lookup_value, table_array, row_index, [range_lookup])					
7	Arnold's Physics Mark		58	=HLOOKUP("Arnold",B1:E4,2,0)		
8	Jomy's Maths Mark		92	=HLOOKUP("Jomy",B1:E4,3,0)		

In this example we are checking how much marks Arnold and Jomy earned in Physics and Maths. There are four parameters we have to supply to HLOOKUP.

First parameter we are searching the name Arnold or Jomy so we will provide the same in double quotes (text should be provided in double quotes).

Second parameter is where we are going to search, since the entire name and mark details are in the range B1:E4 we will provide that as second parameter.

Third parameter we are providing the row number, 2 for Physics 3 for Maths. (Counting from the name row)

Fourth parameter we are entering 0 or False to get an exact match.

Check the example HLOOKUP.XLSX Sheet2

	A	B	C	D	E	F
1	Name	John	Arnold	Jomy	Melvin	
2	Marks in Physics	54	58	84	83	
3	Marks in Maths	65	73	92	80	
4	Marks in Chemistry	51	95	93	55	
5						
6	HLOOKUP (lookup_value, table_array, row_index, [range_lookup])					
7	Physics mark of Student name start with A	58	=HLOOKUP("a*",B1:E4,2,0)			
8	Chemistry mark of Student name start with M	55	=HLOOKUP("melvi?",B1:E4,4,0)			

In this example file we are using the wild card characters. * is used for searching multiple number of characters, m* can be Melvin or Mijo or whatever starts with m. ? means single character, melvi? means Melvin or melvih or melvip. Rest of the entries are same like the previous example.

7.7. HYPERLINK

This function **creates a clickable link.**

Syntax:

=HYPERLINK (link_location, [friendly_name])

Parameter list:

link_location - the path to the file or page to be opened.
friendly_name - [optional] the link text to display in a cell.

Usage notes:

Use the HYPERLINK function to create links to workbook locations, pages on the internet, or to files on network servers.

When a user clicks a cell that contains the HYPERLINK function, Excel will open the file or page specified by link location. Link_location can be a cell reference or named range, a path to a file stored on a local drive, a path a file on a server using Universal Naming Convention (UNC) or a path to a location on the internet or an intranet in Uniform Resource Locator (URL) format.

Points to note.

Link_location should be supplied as a text string in quotation marks or a cell reference that contains the link path as text.

If friendly_name is not supplied, the HYPERLINK will display link_location as the friendly_name.

To select a cell that contains HYPERLINK without jumping to the destination, use arrow keys to select the cell. Alternatively, click on the cell and hold the mouse button down until the cursor changes.

Examples:

=HYPERLINK("http://amazon.com","Click me") will create a link in Excel with the text Click me and if you click the link it will open the site amazon.com.

=HYPERLINK("[C:\My Documents\Report.xlsx]Quarter") will create a hyperlink to an Excel file Report sheet name Quarter.

7.8. INDEX

This function **picks a value in a list or table** by looking down the specified rows and looking across the specified columns.

Syntax:

=INDEX (array, row_num, [col_num], [area_num])

Parameter list:

array - a range of cells, or an array constant.

row_num - the row position in the reference or array.

col_num - [optional] the column position in the reference or array.

area_num - [optional] the range in reference that should be used.

The INDEX function has two forms: Array and Reference.

Array form

In the array form of INDEX, the first parameter is array, which is supplied as a range of cells or an array constant.

Syntax:

INDEX (array, row_num, [col_num])

If both row_num and col_num are supplied, INDEX returns the value in the cell at the intersection of row_num and col_num.

If you row_num is set to zero, INDEX returns an array of values for the entire row. To use these array values, enter the INDEX function as an array formula in horizontal range.

If you col_num is set to zero, INDEX returns an array of values for the entire column. To use these array values, enter the INDEX function as an array formula in vertical range.

Index can be used in so many ways as per the examples given below.

Example 1:

INDEX function with second parameter as row_num.

Check the example file exceltovba.com-INDEX.xlsx (sheet name : Index1).

	A	B	C	D	E
1	Day	Jose	Roy	Ruby	Jomy
2	13	$ 100	$ 250	$ 270	$ 330
3	14	$ 150	$ 230	$ 110	$ 180
4	15	$ 175	$ 160	$ 240	$ 350

In the example file we have to find out the second value In the row using INDEX function. Enter =INDEX(A2:A4,2) so that you will get the second value in the row which is 14, if you want the third row value then you have to enter 3 as the second parameter so that you will get 15 as the answer.

Example 2:

INDEX function with second parameter as col_num.

In the same example file we have to find out the second value in the column using INDEX function. Enter =INDEX(B1:E1,2) so that you will get the second value in the column which is **Roy**, if you want the third column value then you have to enter 3 as the second parameter so that you will get **Ruby** as the answer.

Example 3:

INDEX function with second parameter both row_num and col_num.

Check the example file exceltovba.com-INDEX.xlsx (sheet name : Index2).

In the same example file you have to find out on Day 13 how much Ruby has earned. Enter =INDEX(B2:E4,2,3) in any of the cell and you will get the answer as 110. Instead of hardcoding the row number and column number you can use the cell reference like this =INDEX(B2:E4,E6,E7) and in E6 cell you can give the row number 2 and in E7 column number 3.

So if you want to find out what Jomy has earned on Day 15 you have to just change the value in the cells E6 to 3 and E7 to 4.

	A	B	C	D	E
1	**Day**	**Jose**	**Roy**	**Ruby**	**Jomy**
2	13	$ 100	$ 250	$ 270	$ 330
3	14	$ 150	$ 230	$ 110	$ 180
4	15	$ 175	$ 160	$ 240	$ 350
5					
6	Enter the day (row number)				3
7	Enter the Name (column number)				4
8					
9	Result				350

Reference form

In the reference form of INDEX, the first parameter is reference, which is supplied as a reference to one or more cell ranges.

Syntax:

INDEX (reference, row_num, [col_num], [area_num])

The reference form of INDEX returns the reference of the cell at the intersection row_num and col_num. If reference is supplied as multiple ranges, area_num indicates which range to use. area_sum is supplied as a number.

For example, in the formula =INDEX((A1:D5,A7:D10),2,2,2), area_num is supplied as 2, which refers to the range A7:D10.

You will get the idea once you go through the examples.

Example 4:

Check the example file exceltovba.com-INDEX.xlsx (sheet name : Index3).

This is the advanced version of the Example 3 as there are two groups First (B3:E5) and Second (B9:E11) instead of one group. By including the area_num you can easily check from First or Second group how much each person has earned. You have to enter the formula like this =INDEX((B3:E5,B9:E11),2,3,1) so that you will get the amount earned from the first group as the fourth parameter decides where we have to look, 1 will look in the first group and 2 will look in the second group.

	A	B	C	D	E
1	Day		First Group		
2		Jose	Roy	Ruby	Jomy
3	13	100	250	270	330
4	14	150	230	110	180
5	15	175	160	240	350
6					
7	Day		Second Group		
8		Melvin	Arnold	Roger	Jenni
9	26	220	206	235	256
10	27	173	208	205	278
11	28	440	217	240	299
12					
13	Result using cell ranges				110
15	Formula used		=INDEX((B3:E5,B9:E11),2,3,1)		

Instead of hardcoding the last three parameters you can change it to cell reference so that it will be able easy to manipulate like this =INDEX((B3:E5,B9:E11),E13,E14,E15) ,in the cell E13 you can Type 1 or 2 or 3 for the day, Type 1 or 2 or 3 or 4 for the Name in cell E14, Type 1 for First and 2 for Second group in cell E15.

Check the example file exceltovba.com-INDEX.xlsx (sheet name : Index4).

	A	B	C	D	E
1	Day		First Group		
2		Jose	Roy	Ruby	Jomy
3	1	100	250	270	330
4	2	150	230	110	180
5	3	175	160	240	350
6					
7	Day		Second Group		
8		Melvin	Arnold	Roger	Jenni
9	1	220	206	235	256
10	2	173	208	205	278
11	3	440	217	240	299
12					
13	Type 1 or 2 or 3 for the day				2
14	Type 1 or 2 or 3 or 4 for the Name				3
15	Tyoe 1 for First and 2 for Second group				2
16					
17	Result				205
18	Formula used		=INDEX((B3:E5,B9:E11),E13,E14,E15)		

Also we can make this formula more readable by changing the cell ranges (B3:E5,B9:E11) to a name like FirstandSecond. First select the cell ranges B3:E5,B9:E11 and change the name to FirstandSecond in the cell reference column and then use this name in the formula like this =INDEX(FirstandSecond,E13,E14,E15).

Check the example file exceltovba.com-INDEX.xlsx (sheet name: Index5).

K2

	A	B	C	D	E
1	Day	First Group			
2		Jose	Roy	Ruby	Jomy
3	1	100	250	270	330
4	2	150	230	110	180
5	3	175	160	240	350
6					
7	Day	Second Group			
8		Melvin	Arnold	Roger	Jenni
9	1	220	206	235	256
10	2	173	208	205	278
11	3	440	217	240	299
12					
13	Type 1 or 2 or 3 for the day				2
14	Type 1 or 2 or 3 or 4 for the Name				3
15	Type 1 for First and 2 for Second group				2
16					
17	Result				205
18	Formula used		=INDEX(FirstandSecond,E13,E14,E15)		

Example 5:

This is the advanced version of the previous example. In this we are clubbing together MATCH and IF functions with INDEX to increase the capabilities. Formula is given below and will split the formula for you to understand.

=INDEX(FirstandSecond,MATCH(E13,A3:A5,0),MATCH(E14,B2:E2,0),IF(E15="First",1,IF(E15="Second",2)))

	A	B	C	D	E	F
1	Day		First Month			
2		Melvin	Arnold	Roger	Jenni	
3	13	100	250	270	330	
4	14	150	230	110	180	
5	15	175	160	240	350	
6						
7	Day		Second Month			
8		Melvin	Arnold	Roger	Jenni	
9	13	220	206	235	256	
10	14	173	208	205	278	
11	15	440	217	240	299	
12						
13	Type 1 or 2 or 3 for the day				13	
14	Type 1 or 2 or 3 or 4 for the Name				Arnold	
15	Type 1 for First and 2 for Second group				First	
16						
17	Result				250	
18	Formula used					
19	=INDEX(FirstandSecond,MATCH(E13,A3:A5,0),MATCH(E14,B2:E2,0),					
20	IF(E15="First",1,IF(E15="Second",2)))					

FirstandSecond - First parameter is the name given to the cell range (B3:E5,B9:E11).

MATCH(E13,A3:A5,0) - Second parameter from which we will get the row position of the day we have entered, in this case we will get the return value as 1 as we are checking the position number of the value 13 in the cell range A3:A5.

MATCH(E14,B2:E2,0) – Third parameter from which we will get the column position for the name we have entered, in this case we will get the return value as 2 as we are checking the position number of the value Arnold in the cell range B2:E2.

IF(E15="First",1,IF(E15="Second",2)) – Fourth parameter we are checking whether we have entered the word First or Second in the cell E15. If it is First then IF function will return 1 and if it is Second IF function will return 2 and INDEX function will check the First month if it is 1 and Second month if it is 2.

So after the MATCH and IF function is processed the formula will look like this
=INDEX(FirstandSecond,1,2,1) and you will get the answer 250 which is Arnold earned on the 13th day.

7.9. INDIRECT

This function **creates a cell reference** from a valid worksheet reference.

Syntax:

=INDIRECT (ref_text, [a1])

Parameter list:

ref_text - A reference supplied as text.

a1 - [optional] a boolean (TRUE or FALSE) to indicate A1 or R1C1-style reference. Default is TRUE = A1 style.

Points to note.

Use INDIRECT to create or supply a reference in text form. Indirect is useful when you want to convert a text value into a valid cell reference.

The reference created by INDIRECT will not change even when cells, rows, or columns are inserted or deleted. For example, the formula =INDIRECT("A1:A100") will always refer to the first 100 rows of column A, even If rows In that range are deleted or inserted.

Also if you want to find the sum of values in the cell reference A1:A100 and if the rows are inserted or deleted regularly then you can set the formula like this =SUM(INDIRECT("A1:A100")), it will always give the sum of the A1 to A100. If you directly put a formula like =SUM(A1:A100) you will get error message once the rows are deleted.

In the example file exceltovba.com-INDIRECT.xls (sheet name : Result) we have used the formula =INDIRECT(D1&"!"&D2) to retrieve the value from other sheets. By changing the Sheet name and cell reference you will get the value from the respective sheets.

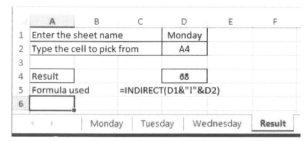

7.10. LOOKUP

Use this function when you need to look in a single row or column and find a value from the same position in a second row or column. There are two ways for this function **Vector form** and **Array form**

Vector Form

Use this form to search one row or one column for a value. We will elaborate using example.

Syntax:

LOOKUP(lookup_value, lookup_vector, [result_vector])

Parameter list:

lookup_value - a value that LOOKUP searches for in the first vector. It can be a number, text, a logical value, or a name or reference that refers to a value. If the LOOKUP function can't find the lookup_value the function returns the value which is less than or equal to lookup_value.

lookup_vector - a range that contains only one row or one column. The values in lookup_vector can be text, numbers, or logical values.

result_vector [Optional] – a range that contains only one row or column. The result_vector argument must be the same size as lookup_vector. It has to be the same size.

Check the example file exceltovba.com-LOOKUP.xlsx Sheet1

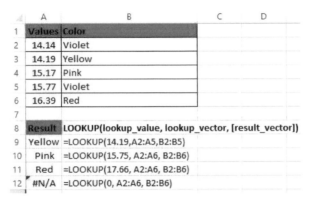

In this example first we are searching for 14.19 in column A and if it matched we are getting the value against column B that is in the same row.

Second we are searching for 15.75 in column A and since it is not matching, matches the nearest smaller value (15.17), and returns the value from column B that is in the same row.

Third we are searching for 17.66 in column A and since it is not matching, matches the nearest smaller value (16.39), and returns the value from column B that is in the same row.

Looks up 0 in column A, and returns an error because 0 is less than the smallest value (14.14) in column A.

Points to note.

The values in lookup_vector must be placed in ascending order: ..., -2, -1, 0, 1, 2, ..., A-Z, FALSE, TRUE; otherwise, LOOKUP might not return the correct value.

Lookup is not case sensitive, Uppercase and lowercase text are equivalent.

If lookup_value is smaller than the smallest value in lookup_vector, LOOKUP returns the #N/A error value.

Array form

This form of LOOKUP is provided for compatibility with other spreadsheet programs, but its functionality is limited, instead you can use VLOOKUP or HLOOKUP.

The array form of LOOKUP is very similar to the HLOOKUP and VLOOKUP functions. The difference is that HLOOKUP searches for the value of lookup_value in the first row, VLOOKUP searches in the first column, and LOOKUP searches according to the dimensions of array. The limitation of the LOOKUP function is you will always get the last value in the row or column, you cannot get the in-between values.

So you must use VLOOKUP or HLOOKUP.

7.11. MATCH

This function **searches for specified item in a range of cells and returns the relative position** of that item in the range. For example, if the range A1:A3 contains the values 8, 39, and 54, then the formula

=MATCH(39,A1:A3,0) returns the number 2, 39 is the second item in the range.

Syntax:

=MATCH (lookup_value, lookup_array, [match_type])

Parameter list:

lookup_value - the value to match in lookup_array.
lookup_array - a range of cells or an array reference.
match_type - [optional] How to match, specified as -1, 0, or 1. Default is 1.

Match type information

If match_type is 1, MATCH finds the largest value that Is less than or equal to lookup_value. The lookup_array must be sorted in ascending order.
If match_type is 0, MATCH finds the first value exactly equal to lookup_value. lookup_array does not need to be sorted.
If match_type is -1, MATCH finds the smallest value that is greater than or equal to lookup_value. The lookup_array must be sorted in descending order.
If match_type is omitted, it is assumed to be 1.

Points to note.

Match is not case-sensitive.
Match returns the #N/A error if no match is found
If match_type is 0 and lookup_value is text, lookup_value can contain the wildcard characters asterisk (*) and question mark (?). An asterisk matches any sequence of characters; a question mark matches any single character.

Example1:

Check the example file exceltovba.com-MATCH.xlsx Sheet1

	A	B	C	D	E
1	Names	Marks			
2	Raj	30			
3	Melvin	40			
4	John	50			
5	Arnold	60			
6					
7	MATCH (lookup_value, lookup_array, [match_type])				
8	Type a name	Melvin			
9	The position is	2			
10		=MATCH(B7,B2:B5)			
11					
12	Type the marks	50			
13	The postion is	3			
14		=MATCH(B11,C2:C5)			

In this example first we are finding out the position of the name Melvin from these four names as you can see Melvin is in second position and we will get the answer as 2 and in the marks 50 is in 3rd position out of the four marks mentioned so we will get the answer as 3.

Example2:

Check the example file exceltovba.com-MATCH.xlsx Sheet2 using match_type 0

	A	B	C	D	E
1	Ascending		Descending		Wrong Value
2	10		40		10
3	20		30		20
4	30		20		30
5	40		10		40
6					
7	MATCH (lookup_value, lookup_array, [match_type])				
8	20		20		25
9	2		3		#N/A
10	=MATCH(A8,A2:A5,0)		=MATCH(C8,C2:C5,0)		=MATCH(E8,E2:E5,0)

In this example file we are using match_type 0 as third parameter for exact match so it is not mandatory to sort the list and the function will check only exact match , if it is not matched the #NA error is returned.

You can see the ascending and descending list gives the exact match.

The Wrong Value list cannot find an exact match, so the #NA error is returned.

Example2:

Check the example file exceltovba.com-MATCH.xlsx Sheet3 using match_type 1

	A	B	C	D	E
1	Ascending		Descending		Wrong Value
2	10		40		10
3	20		30		20
4	30		20		30
5	40		10		40
6					
7	MATCH (lookup_value, lookup_array, [match_type])				
8	20		20		25
9	2		#N/A		2
10	=MATCH(A8,A2:A5,1)		=MATCH(C8,C2:C5,1)		=MATCH(E8,E2:E5,1)

In this example file we are using match_type 1 as third parameter to find the exact match or less than lookup_value. If you are using the match_type 1 as third parameter then the list should be ascending order otherwise it will return #NA error.
So the Ascending list gives the exact match and the Descending list gives the #NA error.
The Wrong Value list finds the next lowest number because there is no exact match for the value 25 and since the list is in ascending order it will find next lowest number which is 20.

Example3:

Check the example file exceltovba.com-MATCH.xlsx Sheet4 using match_type -1

	A	B	C	D	E
1	Ascending		Descending		Wrong Value
2	10		40		10
3	20		30		20
4	30		20		30
5	40		10		40
6					
7	MATCH (lookup_value, lookup_array, [match_type])				
8	20		20		25
9	#N/A		3		#N/A
10	=MATCH(A8,A2:A5,-1)		=MATCH(C8,C2:C5,-1)		=MATCH(E8,E2:E5,-1)

In this example file we are using match_type -1 as third parameter to finds the exact match or greater than lookup_value. The list should be sorted in descending order
The Ascending list gives the #NA error.
The Descending list gives the exact match.
The Wrong Value list finds the next highest number but because it in ascending order it will return #NA error.

7.12. OFFSET

This function **creates a reference offset from given starting point** and returns a cell reference. The starting point can be one cell or a range of cells, and the offset is supplied as rows or columns "offset" from the starting point. The height and width arguments are optional and determine the size of the reference that is created.

Syntax:

=OFFSET (reference, rows, cols, [height], [width])

Parameter list:

reference - the starting point, supplied as a cell reference or range.
rows - the number of rows to offset below the starting reference.
cols - the number of columns to offset to the right of the starting reference.
height - [optional] The height in rows of the returned reference.
width - [optional] The width in columns of the returned reference.

Check the example file exceltovba.com-OFFSET.xlsx

	A	B	C	D
1	Result	OFFSET (reference, rows, cols, [height], [width])		
2	18	=OFFSET(C1,3,0)		
3	74	=OFFSET(B2,2,2)	9	85
4	194	=SUM(OFFSET(A2,1,3,3,1))	18	74
5			16	35
6				

In this example first we are getting the value 18 by offsetting from cell reference C1, 3 rows down and 0 column (same column).

Like that we are getting the value 74 by offsetting from the cell B2, 2 rows down and 2 columns right.

And last we are calculating the sum of the cell range D3:D5. First we are offsetting from A2 cell 1 row down and 3 column right to reach the cell reference. Fourth and Fifth parameters specify the rows and columns to include. Fourth parameter is 3 so it will include 3 rows from D3 and only include 1 column (fifth parameter is 1).

Points to note.

OFFSET can be used to build a dynamic named range for charts or pivot tables, to make sure that source data is always up to date.

OFFSET only returns a reference, no cells or moved.
Both rows and cols can be supplied as negative numbers to reverse their normal offset direction - negative cols offset to the left, and negative rows offset above.
OFFSET is a "volatile" formula; it is recalculated whenever there is any change to a worksheet. It can slow down Excel in a complicated worksheet.
OFFSET will display the #REF! error value if the offset is outside the edge of the worksheet.

When height or width is omitted, the height and width of reference is used.
OFFSET can be used with any other function that expects to receive a reference.

7.13. ROW

This function **returns the row number** of a reference. If you have given a cell range then it will return the first cell range row number. So =ROW(B2) will return 2 and =ROW(C2:C9) will also return 2 since it will return only the first row number of the range. If you enter the formula without arguments like this =ROW() in a cell it will return the row number of the particular cell you have entered the function.

Syntax:

=ROW ([reference])

Parameter list:

reference – [optional] a reference to a cell or range of cells.

7.14. ROWS

This function returns the number of rows in an array or reference.

Syntax:

=ROWS (array)

Parameter list:

array - reference to a cell or range of cells.

Use ROWS to get the row count of a reference. For example, the formula =ROWS(A1:A10) returns the number 10 as there are 10 rows in this range from A1 to A10.

7.15. TRANSPOSE

This function converts vertical range of cell to horizontal and horizontal range of cells to vertical and returns an array in a new orientation. Since this is an array function you have to press Ctrl+Shift+Enter after selecting and entering this formula to the cells you want the new values to be pasted.

Syntax:

=TRANSPOSE (array)

Parameter list:

array - the array or range of cells to transpose.

The new array must occupy the same number of rows as the source array has columns, and the same number of columns as the source array has rows.

Check the example file exceltovba.com-OFFSET.xlsx

	A	B	C	D	E	F	G	H	I	J
1	Name	Physics	Maths	Chemistry		Name	John	Arnold	Jomy	Melvin
2	John	54	65	51		Physics	54	58	84	83
3	Arnold	58	73	95		Maths	65	73	92	80
4	Jomy	84	92	93		Chemistry	51	95	93	55
5	Melvin	83	80	55						

In this example first we have to select the cell range F1:J4 (you should select the 5 columns as there are 5 rows to convert and you should select 4 rows as there are 4 columns to convert).

Enter the formula =TRANSPOSE(A1:D5) and press Ctrl+Shift+Enter to convert to array formula and the columns and rows will get transposed.

7.16. VLOOKUP

Vlookup is one of the versatile and powerful formulas in Excel and is used extensively for **comparing excel sheets, data extracting** etc. Vlookup means Vertical lookup. This function searches the value you provide in a table or cell ranges (searches in the table's first column) and returns the value in the same row according to the column number you specify.

Syntax:

VLOOKUP(lookup_value, table_array, col_index_num, [range_lookup])

Parameter list:

Lookup_value - the value to search for, like if you want to search the name John is available in other list then you will select the cell with the name John.
table_array - where we are going to search, it will definitely be a group of cells or table in same sheet or other sheet or other workbook.
col_index_num - the column number in the table from which to retrieve a value.
range_lookup - [optional] TRUE = approximate match (default). FALSE = exact match.

Right now the parameters looks confusing but don't worry once I explain using examples you will find it very easy.

Vlookup using the range lookup FALSE.

Example 1:

Check the example file exceltovba.com-VLOOKUP1.xlsx

In this example we want to find the marks earned by each Students.

First we are going to search the name John in the cell range C7:F10, so first we enter the name John as first parameter in double quotes as we are searching a text, and second parameter we are entering the cell range C7:F10 where we are going to search.

Third parameter we are specifying the column index number from the cell range C7:F10 since the starting column is C it is the first column number, D the second column number, E the third one and F the fourth one. And fourth parameter we are putting 0 or False to get an exact match.

The point to be noted here is the cell range C7:F10 the C column (first column) must have the value John what we are searching, then only VLOOKUP will work otherwise it will give a #N/A error.

In this example we are hardcoding the value we are searching and this is not and efficient way. So we will make some change to make the life easier in the second Example.

	A	B	C	D	E	F	G	H	I
1				**Third parameter**					
2				col_index_num					
3									
4			↓	↓	↓	↓			
5			1	2	3	4			
6			Name	Physics	Maths	Chemistry			
7			John	54	65	51			
8	First Parameter		Arnold	58	73	95			
9	lookup_value		Jomy	84	92	93			
10			Melvin	83	80	55			
11									
12			John's Physics mark				54	=VLOOKUP("John",C7:F10,2,0)	
13			Arnold's Maths mark				73	=VLOOKUP("Arnold",C7:F10,3,0)	
14			Jomy's Chemistry mark				93	=VLOOKUP("Jomy",C7:F10,4,0)	
15									
16				**Second Parameter**					
17				table_array - cell range C7:F10					

Points to note.

VLOOKUP only looks from left to the right, in this case if the Name column (C) comes after the Chemistry column (F) then this function won't work, either you have to copy the name column to the left hand side or you can use the functions INDEX and MATCH clubbed together to overcome this limitation.

VLOOKUP will always look for the first match only. If there are two persons with same name then VLOOKUP will retrieve the first value only. In the above example if there is one more person whose name is John then you won't be able to retrieve the data of that person.

VLOOKUP is not case sensitive, the name John or JOHN or JoHn is treated as same.

If you change the cell range by inserting or deleting the columns then the VLOOKUP value will give wrong answer. In the above example if you delete the Physics column then Maths column will become the second column and you will get a wrong answer.

Sometimes data you see will look like a number but it may be formatted as text. In this case you have change the text to number using the VALUE function.

You will get #N/A error if the data you are searching is not there. If the name John is not there then you will get this error.

Also if you enter the wrong col_index_num you will get out of reference error like this #REF!. In the above example if you enter 7 as the third parameter you will get this error as there are only four columns to retrieve data.

Before writing the Vlookup formula you must check the data columns you are comparing does not contain any leading and trailing space as this will give wrong results as the data you are seeing and actual data may be of different length. Say if the name you are seeing is John but the data length may be five because of the trailing or leading space. In such cases you have to use the trim function to eliminate these spaces.

Example 2:

Check the example file exceltovba.com-VLOOKUP2.xlsx

In this example instead of hardcoding the first and third parameters we are supplying the same as cell references E7 and E8 so that you can change the name and the column number in the respective cells to get the results easily. Also if you want you can give a name to the cell range like Marks or Totalmarks so the formula will be easy to read like this =VLOOKUP(F7,Marks,F8,0).

	A	B	C	D	E	F
1			Name	Physics	Maths	Chemistry
2			John	54	65	51
3			Arnold	58	73	95
4			Jomy	84	92	93
5			Melvin	83	80	55
6						
7	Enter the name					Arnold
8	Enter 2 for Physics, 3 for Math, 4 for Chemistry					4
9						
10	Result					95
11						
12	Formula used		=VLOOKUP(F7,C2:F5,F8,0)			

Example 3:

Clubbing VLOOKUP with MATCH for a fully dynamic column index

Check the example file exceltovba.com-VLOOKUP3.xlsx

	A	B	C	D	E	F	G	H	I
1	Company	Spare parts	Cost						
2	Ford	Filters	120	=VLOOKUP(B2,$A$17:$F$21,MATCH(A2,$B$16:$F$16,0)+1,0)					
3	Audi	Suspension	850	=VLOOKUP(B3,$A$17:$F$21,MATCH(A3,$B$16:$F$16,0)+1,0)					
4	BMW	Engine	842	=VLOOKUP(B4,$A$17:$F$21,MATCH(A4,$B$16:$F$16,0)+1,0)					
5	Nissan	Exhaust	589	=VLOOKUP(B5,$A$17:$F$21,MATCH(A5,$B$16:$F$16,0)+1,0)					
6	Peugeot	Gear Box	700	=VLOOKUP(B6,$A$17:$F$21,MATCH(A6,$B$16:$F$16,0)+1,0)					
7	Nissan	Engine	477	=VLOOKUP(B7,$A$17:$F$21,MATCH(A7,$B$16:$F$16,0)+1,0)					
8	Ford	Suspension	285	=VLOOKUP(B8,$A$17:$F$21,MATCH(A8,$B$16:$F$16,0)+1,0)					
9	Audi	Exhaust	667	=VLOOKUP(B9,$A$17:$F$21,MATCH(A9,$B$16:$F$16,0)+1,0)					
10	Peugeot	Gear Box	700	=VLOOKUP(B10,$A$17:$F$21,MATCH(A10,$B$16:$F$16,0)+1,0)					
11	BMW	Engine	842	=VLOOKUP(B11,$A$17:$F$21,MATCH(A11,$B$16:$F$16,0)+1,0)					
12	Nissan	Suspension	521	=VLOOKUP(B12,$A$17:$F$21,MATCH(A12,$B$16:$F$16,0)+1,0)					
13									

	Cost Table					
14						
15			Company			
16	Spare Parts	Ford	Audi	BMW	Nissan	Peugeot
17	Filters	120	744	653	698	888
18	Gear Box	450	550	600	596	700
19	Engine	981	974	842	477	469
20	Exhaust	863	667	340	589	922
21	Suspension	285	850	899	521	362

In this example file we are clubbing VLOOKUP with MATCH to create a dynamic VLOOKUP so that we can compare data vertically and horizontally in a single go. In the first and second parameter of the VLOOKUP we are checking the spare part name is available in Cost Table and if it is there we will fetch the data according to the column number derived from MATCH function.

As third parameter we are entering the MATCH function like this MATCH(A2,$B$16:$F$16,0)+1. What this means is we are matching the company name and if it matches the cost will be picked from the particular column and in order to give the exact column name we should add 1 to match value to give the VLOOKUP the correct column number as VLOOKUP starts comparing from COLUMN A.

Here we are adding the dollar sign in the second and third parameter in order to lock the cell range we are looking so that when you copy down the formula VLOOKUP will still search the same Cost table.

Vlookup with Range_lookup True

Another great use of Vlookup is to automatically categorize the data according to your specification. Say if you want to award grades to the students in the school according to the marks they earned or if you want to categorize the sales person according to their performance you can make use of this property.

Example 4:

Check the example file exceltovba.com-VLOOKUP4.xlsx

In this file we are finding out students Grades according to the Grade Criteria you have created. The main thing to remember is the first column of the Grade Criteria should be in ascending order otherwise it will give wrong results and F column is added for you to see the Grades visually and is not required for calculation.

Formula used =VLOOKUP(B2,$E$2:$G$7,3,TRUE)

	A	B	C	D	E	F	G
1	Name	Physics	Grade		Grades Criteria		
2	John	99	A		Marks between		Grades
3	Arnold	58	E		0	49	Failed
4	Jomy	80	B		50	59	E
5	Melvin	71	C		60	69	D
6	Ron	15	Failed		70	79	C
7	Roger	64	D		80	89	B
8	Helen	49	Failed		90	100	A
9	Jim	58	E				
10	Denis	30	Failed		Formula used		
11	Lopez	90	A	=VLOOKUP(B2,$E$3:$G$8,3,TRUE)			
12	Miranda	77	C				
13	Michale	64	D				
14	Ausin	41	Failed				
15	Jay	83	B				

First we are comparing B column with the E column and then get the corresponding row value in the G Column. So first we compare the John's mark , the VLOOKUP will check whether the value 99 is there in the Grades criteria column E and if it doesn't find it will fall back to the next value which is 90 and since we have given the third parameter as 3 it will pick from the third column which is A.

Likewise for Arnold it will check 58 is there, if it is not there it will fall back to the next value which is 50 and we will get the Grade E and if you copy the whole formula down you will get the grades for all students.

Points to note.

We have used TRUE as the fourth parameter, you can use 1 instead or else you can omit this because by default the fourth parameter is TRUE.

As you can see in the second parameter we have used dollar sign in-between the cell reference, this is used to change the cell reference from relative to absolute. In other words this is used for locking the cells so that when you copy down the VLOOKUP formula it should always search inside the cell range E3 to G8. Try copying down without the dollar sign and see what happens.

If the Grades Criteria is in separate workbook then you don't have to put the Dollar sign it will automatically inserted into the formula otherwise you can manually enter by hitting the F4 key after entering the second criteria.

How to handle the Errors

Say if you want to VLOOKUP the data and based on the VLOOKUP data you want to perform some calculations. In the first example if John is not there then we will get #N/A Error and whatever calculations you are going to do will go wrong.

In this case you should go for one more error checking function ISNA function. It basically tests #N/A Error and returns TRUE, otherwise the function returns FALSE. So I will add one more layer to the first VLOOKUP formula, before the VLOOKUP we will add ISNA like this.

=ISNA (VLOOKUP(A2,Sheet2!$B$2:$C$9,2,0))

So this function will return True if #N/A Error is there and False if not. But still if you want to do some calculations it won't be of any use if we get the answer as True or False. So I am adding one more layer if the value Is there we should get the value otherwise we should get 0. For that you can use the IF formula. Hope you remember the formula.

If (logical test, value if true, value if wrong)

In the first parameter we will put the formula

=ISNA (VLOOKUP(A2,Sheet2!$B$2:$C$9,2,0))

and if this is true then we should get 0 so we will put 0 as second parameter and in the third parameter again we will write the same Vlookup formula without ISNA function like this VLOOKUP(A2,Sheet2!$B$2:$C$9,2,0) so that you should get the answer if the value is present . So if you club all three parameters the formula will look like this.

=IF(ISNA(VLOOKUP(A2,Sheet2!$B$2:$C$9,2,0)),0, (VLOOKUP(A2,Sheet2!$B$2:$C$9,2,0)))

Points to consider when using VLOOKUP.

VLOOKUP cannot lookup to the left of the column, if the data you are looking is on the left side of the table you are looking then you won't be able to get the details.

Also if you are doing VLOOKUP for large chunks of data then it will slow down the Excel considerably. In this case you can use the INDEX and MATCH function clubbed together to behave like VLOOKUP function.

8. Math and Trigonometry

8.1. ABS

This functions **returns the absolute value of a number.**

Syntax:

ABS(number)

Parameter list:

number - the real number of which you want the absolute value.

As you can see it removes all the negative sign from the numbers as in the example given below.

	A	B	C
1	Numbers	ABS	Formula used
2	-560	560	=ABS(B1)
3	-98.654	98.654	=ABS(B2)
4	-45	45	=ABS(B3)

Check the example file exceltovba.com-ABS.xls

Please open sheet2 in the same example file and here we are finding the total of all the values in B column irrespective of the sign be it positive or negative.

	A	B	C
1		Values	
2		-25	
3		65	
4		-75	
5		105	
6		-95	
7		-100	
8		35	
9			
10	Total	-90	=SUM(B2:B8)
11	Total using ABS	500	{=SUM(ABS(B2:B8))}
12	Total using ABS	500	=SUMPRODUCT(ABS(B2:B9))

Here you can see in the B10 cell we have calculated the total sum, SUM function will adjust the positive and negative values you will get the difference of positive and negative values. But if you want to get the total of all irrespective of the sign then we will use this formula =SUM(ABS(B2:B8)) and press Ctrl+Shift+Enter so that this formula will be changed to array formula like this {=SUM(ABS(B2:B8))} and you will get the SUM of all the values irrespective of the sign.

What this formula does is it will create an array in the memory with absolute values and then add up all the values to give back the SUM.

If you don't want to use array formula you can use the formula like this =SUMPRODUCT(ABS(B2:B9)). SUMPRODUCT usually multiplies the arrays and will make a total of the multiplied values. Since here there is only one array B2:B9 SUMPRODUCT function will just add up all the value after converting to absolute values and you will get the total of the same.

8.2. AGGREGATE

This is a new function introduced in Excel 2010 and is very versatile function, so **many functions clubbed together to this single function**. The aggregate function can be used as SUM, COUNT, MIN, AVERAGE depends upon the function_num you specify. =AGGREGATE(9,0,A1:A2) will find the SUM of the cells A1 and A2, =AGGREGATE(1,0,A1:A2) will find the AVERAGE of the cells A1 and A2.

There are two forms for this function **Reference** form and **Array** form

REFERENCE FORM

Syntax:

AGGREGATE(function_num, options, ref1, [ref2], ...)

function_num - a number 1 through 13 to specify the function, as shown in the function_num Table below.
options - a number that determines which values to ignore in the evaluation range for the function, as shown in the options Table below.
ref1 - the first reference or numeric argument for which you want the aggregate value.
ref2 [Optional]. references or numeric arguments 2 to 253 for which you want the aggregate value.

ARRAY FORM

Syntax:

AGGREGATE(function_num, options, array, [k])

function_num - a number from 14 to 19 that specifies which function, as shown in the function_num Table below.
options - a number that determines which values to ignore in the evaluation range for the function, as shown in the Options Table below.
array - an array, an array formula, or a reference to a range of cells for which you want the aggregate value.
k - each of the six Array-Form functions (LARGE, SMALL, PERCENTILE.INC, QUARTILE.INC, PERCENTILE.EXC and QUARTILE.EXC requires a second argument.

Points to note.

The function will not ignore hidden rows, nested subtotals or nested aggregates if the array argument includes a calculation, for example: =AGGREGATE(14,3,A1:A10*(A1:A10>0),1)

If a second ref argument is required but not provided, AGGREGATE returns a #VALUE! error.
If one or more of the references are 3-D references, AGGREGATE returns the #VALUE! error value.
The AGGREGATE function is designed for columns of data, or vertical ranges.

Function_num Table

Function_num	Function	Syntax Form
1	AVERAGE	Reference
2	COUNT	Reference
3	COUNTA	Reference
4	MAX	Reference
5	MIN	Reference
6	PRODUCT	Reference
7	STDEV.S	Reference
8	STDEV.P	Reference
9	SUM	Reference
10	VAR.S	Reference
11	VAR.P	Reference
12	MEDIAN	Reference
13	MODE.SNGL	Reference
14	LARGE	Array
15	SMALL	Array
16	PERCENTILE.INC	Array
17	QUARTILE.INC	Array
18	PERCENTILE.EXC	Array
19	QUARTILE.EXC	Array

Second parameter Options is a numerical value that determines which values to ignore from the range you specify. Details of the option number and their behavior given below.

Options Table

Option	Behavior
0 or omitted	Ignore nested SUBTOTAL and AGGREGATE functions
1	Ignore hidden rows, nested SUBTOTAL and AGGREGATE functions
2	Ignore error values, nested SUBTOTAL and AGGREGATE functions
3	Ignore hidden rows, error values, nested SUBTOTAL and AGGREGATE functions
4	Ignore nothing
5	Ignore hidden rows
6	Ignore error values
7	Ignore hidden rows and error values

Check the example file exceltovba.com-AGGREGATE.xlsx

	A	B	C
4	35	97	
5	#NUM!	65	
6	29	51	
7	101	72	
8	45	54	
9	88	81	
10	39	99	
11	58	95	
12	38	85	
13			
14	Result	AGGREGATE(function_num, options, ref1, [ref2], ...)	
15	101	=AGGREGATE(4, 6, A2:A12)	
16	68.5	=AGGREGATE(12, 6, A2:A12, B2:B12)	
17			
18		AGGREGATE(function_num, options, array, [k])	
19	#VALUE!	=AGGREGATE(15, 6, A2:A12)	
20	35	=AGGREGATE(15,6,A2:B12,2)	
21	75	=AGGREGATE(14, 6, A2:A12, 3)	

In this example we are first calculating the maximum value while ignoring error values in the range. =AGGREGATE(4, 6, A2:A12). First parameter in this function is 6 so this function will calculate MAX value while ignoring the error values which is specified in the second parameter as 6 from the range supplied.

Second we are calculating the median while ignoring error values in the range.

And the last three we are using the array form.

Third we are getting a #VALUE! error because AGGREGATE is expecting (function SMALL) a second ref argument, it is an array form, so you should provide the fourth parameter.
Fourth one calculates the 2nd smallest item while ignoring error values in the range.
Fifth one calculates the 3rd largest value while ignoring error values in the range.

8.3. CEILING

This function **rounds a number up away from zero** to the nearest specified multiple and return value will be a rounded number.

Syntax:

=CEILING (number, significance)

Parameter list:

number - the number you want to round.

significance - the multiple to which you want to round.

Points to note.

If either argument is nonnumeric, CEILING returns the #VALUE! error value.

Regardless of the sign of number, a value is rounded up when adjusted away from zero. If number is an exact multiple of significance, no rounding occurs.

If number is negative, and significance is negative, the value is rounded down, away from zero.

If number is negative, and significance is positive, the value is rounded up towards zero.

Examples:

=CEILING(5.5, 1)   Rounds 5.5 up to nearest multiple of 1 which is 6.
=CEILING(-5.5, -2)   Rounds -5.5 up to nearest multiple of -2 which is -6.
=CEILING(-5.5, 2)   Rounds -5.5 up to nearest multiple of 2 which is -4.
=CEILING(6.5, 0.1)   Rounds 6.5 up to the nearest multiple of 0.1 which is 6.5.
=CEILING(0.586, 0.01)   Rounds 0.586 up to the nearest multiple of 0.01 which is 0.59.

8.4. CEILING.PRECISE

This function returns a number that is rounded up to the nearest integer or to the nearest multiple of significance. Regardless of the sign of the number, the number is rounded up and if the number or the significance is zero, zero is returned.

Syntax::

CEILING.PRECISE(number, [significance])

Parameter list:

number - the value to be rounded.
Significance [optional] - the multiple to which number is to be rounded. If significance is omitted, its default value is 1.

Examples:

=CEILING.PRECISE(8.3)   Rounds 8.3 up to the nearest multiple of 1 which is 9.
=CEILING.PRECISE(-8.3) Rounds -8.3 up to the nearest multiple of 1, rounds toward 0 because the number is negative and we will get the answer -8.
=CEILING.PRECISE(8.3, 2) Rounds 8.3 up to the nearest multiple of 2 which is 10.
=CEILING.PRECISE(8.3,-2) Rounds 8.3 up to the nearest multiple of -2 which is 10.
=CEILING.PRECISE(-8.3,2) Rounds -8.3 up to the nearest multiple of 2, rounds toward 0 because the number is negative and we will get the answer -8.
=CEILING.PRECISE(-8.3,-2) Rounds -8.3 up to the nearest multiple of -2 and we will get -8.

8.5. COMBIN

This function **returns the number of combinations** for a given number of items.

COMBIN(number, number_chosen)

Parameter list:

number - the number of items.
number_chosen - the number of items in each combination.

For example =COMBIN(6, 2) we will get the answer as 15 as there are 15 combinations we can make without the duplicate entry. For any 6 objects (eg. p, q, r, s, t, u) there are 15 different combinations of 2 objects. These are: pq, pr, ps, pt, pu, qr, qs, qt, qu, rs, rt, ru, st, su, tu.

Points to note.

If either argument Number or Number_chosen is nonnumeric, COMBIN returns the #VALUE! error value.
If number < 0 or number_chosen < 0 or number < number_chosen COMBIN returns the #NUM! error value.

8.6. EVEN

This function **rounds a number up to the next even integer** and returns an even integer.

Syntax:

=EVEN (number)

Parameter list:

number - the number to round up to an even integer.

Points to note.

If number is nonnumeric, EVEN returns the #VALUE! error value.
The negative numbers are rounded "up" away from zero, so they actually become more negative.

Examples:

=EVEN(4.5)	Rounds 4.5 to the nearest even integer 6.
=EVEN(5)	Rounds 5 to the nearest even Integer 6.
=EVEN(4)	Rounds 4 to the nearest even integer 4.
=EVEN(-3)	Rounds -3 to the nearest even integer -4.

8.7. EXP

This function finds the **value of e raised to the power of a number**. The constant e equals 2.71828182845904, the base of the natural logarithm.

Syntax:

=EXP (number)

Parameter list:

number - the power that e is raised to.

Examples:

=EXP(1) we will get the approximate value of **e** which is 2.71828183
=EXP(2) we will get the base of the natural logarithm **e** raised to the power of 2 which is 7.3890561.

8.8. FACT

This function **finds the factorial of a number**. The factorial of a number is equal to 1*2*...* number. For example factorial of 4 is 1 x2x3x4 which is 24.

Syntax:

=FACT (number)

Parameter list:

number - the number to get the factorial of.

Points to note.

The number must not be negative or you will get an error value.
If the number is not an integer it will be truncated.

Examples:

=FACT(4)	Factorial of 4, or 1*2*3*4 is 24.
=FACT(2.9)	Factorial of the integer of 2.9 is 2.
=FACT(0)	Factorial of 0 is 1.
=FACT(-5)	Factorial of a negative number returns an error value #NUM!.
=FACT(1)	Factorial of 1 is 1.

8.9. FACTDOUBLE

This function **returns the double factorial** of a number.

Syntax:

FACTDOUBLE(number)

Parameter list:

number - the value for which to return the double factorial. If number is not an integer, it is truncated.

Points to note.

If number is nonnumeric, FACTDOUBLE returns the #VALUE! error value.
If number is negative, FACTDOUBLE returns the #NUM! error value.
If number is even it will multiply all the even numbers to the number.
If number is odd it will multiply all the odd numbers to the number.

Examples:

=FACTDOUBLE(4) because 4 is an even number the double factorial is equivalent to 4*2 and we will get 8 as the answer.
=FACTDOUBLE(6) because 6 is an even number the double factorial is equivalent to 6*4*2 and we will get 48 as the answer
=FACTDOUBLE(5) because 5 is an odd number the double factorial is equivalent to 5*3 and we will get 15 as the answer.
=FACTDOUBLE(7) because 7 is an odd number the double factorial is equivalent to 7*5*3 and we will get 105 as the answer.

8.10. FLOOR

This function **will round a number down to the nearest specified multiple** and returns a rounded number.

Syntax:

=FLOOR (number, multiple)

Parameter list:

number - the number that should be rounded.
multiple - the multiple to use when rounding.

Points to note.

If either of the parameters Is nonnumeric, FLOOR returns the #VALUE! error value.
If number is positive and significance is negative, FLOOR returns the #NUM! error value.
If the sign of number is negative the value Is rounded down and adjusted away from zero. If number is an exact multiple of significance, no rounding occurs.

Examples:

=FLOOR(5.7,2)   Rounds 5.7 down to nearest multiple of 2 which is 4.
=FLOOR(-5.5,-2) Rounds -5.5 down to nearest multiple of -2 which is -4.
=FLOOR(2.5,-2) Returns an error value, because 2.5 and -2 have different signs #NUM!.
=FLOOR(2.58,0.1) Rounds 2.58 down to the nearest multiple of 0.1 which is 2.5.
=FLOOR(0.334,0.01) Rounds 0.334 down to the nearest multiple of 0.01 which is 0.33.

8.11. FLOOR.PRECISE

This function **returns a number that is rounded down to the nearest integer** or to the nearest multiple of significance. It ignores the sign of the number and the number is rounded down. However, if the number or the significance is zero, zero is returned.

Syntax:

FLOOR.PRECISE(number, [significance])

Parameter list:

number - the value to be rounded.
significance [optional] the multiple to which number is to be rounded. If significance is omitted, its default value is 1.

Examples:

=FLOOR.PRECISE(-6.2,-1) rounds -6.2 down to the nearest multiple of -1 to -7.
=FLOOR.PRECISE(6.2, 1) rounds 6.2 down to the nearest multiple of 1 to 6.
=FLOOR.PRECISE(-6.2, 1) rounds -6.2 down to the nearest multiple of 1 to -7.
=FLOOR.PRECISE(6.2,-1) rounds 6.2 down to the nearest multiple of -1 to 6.
=FLOOR.PRECISE(6.2) rounds 6.2 down to nearest multiple of 1   to 6.

8.12. GCD

This function **returns the greatest common divisor** of two or more numbers. The greatest common divisor is the largest integer that divides both number1 and number2 without a remainder.

Syntax:

=GCD (number1, [number2], ...)

Parameter list:

number1 - the first number.
number2 - [optional] the second number.

The GCD function can accept up to 255 numbers as arguments.

Examples:

=GCD(7, 2)   Greatest common divisor of 7 and 2 is 1.
=GCD(36, 44)   Greatest common divisor of 36 and 44 is 4.
=GCD(7, 1)   Greatest common divisor of 7 and 1 is 1.
=GCD(7, 0)   Greatest common divisor of 7 and 0 is 7.

8.13. INT

This function **rounds the number to the integer by rounding down**. For example, INT (8.99) returns the number 8 and INT(-9.8) will give you more negative number -10 as INT function will always round down.

Syntax:

=INT (number)

Parameter list:

number - the number from which you want an integer.

TRUNC and INT are similar functions. TRUNC removes the fractional part of the number. INT rounds numbers down to the nearest integer based on the value of the fractional part of the number. INT and

TRUNC are different only when using negative numbers; TRUNC(-8.3) returns -8 but INT(-8.3) returns -9 because -9 is the lowest number.

8.14. LCM

This function **returns the least common multiple** of the number or numbers.

Syntax:

=LCM (number1, [number2], ...)

Parameter list:

number1 - the first number.
number2 - [optional] the second number.

Use the LCM function when you want to calculate the least common multiple of integers. The least common multiple is the smallest positive integer that is a multiple of all of the numbers supplied as arguments.

For example, =LCM(3,4) returns 12, since 12 is the smallest multiple of both 3 and 4. However, =LCM(3,4,5) returns 60, since 60 is the smallest multiple of all three numbers.

Points to note.

If any argument is nonnumeric, LCM returns the #VALUE! error value.
If any argument Is less than zero, LCM returns the #NUM! error value.

8.15. MOD

This function returns the remainder from division.

Syntax:

=MOD (number, divisor)

Parameter list:

number - the number for which you want to find the remainder.
divisor - the number by which you want to divide number.

=MOD(16,4) you will get 0 as reminder as 16 is completely divisible by 4.
=MOD(35,3) you will get 2, 3 x 11 is 33 and the difference between 35 and 33 is 2.

8.16. MROUND

This function will **round a number to the nearest specified multiple**. MROUND rounds up, away from zero. The rounding happens when dividing number by multiple is greater than or equal to half the value of multiple.

Syntax:

=MROUND (number, multiple)

Parameter list:

number - The number that should be rounded.
multiple - The multiple to use when rounding.

=MROUND(11, 3)	Rounds 11 to the nearest multiple of 3 which is 12.
=MROUND(-7, -3)	Rounds -7 to the nearest multiple of -3 which is -6.
=MROUND(2.3, 0.2)	Rounds 2.3 to the nearest multiple of 0.2 which is 2.4.
=MROUND(10, -3)	Returns the #NUM! error message because -3 and 10 have different signs and

will get #NUM!

8.17. ODD

This function **round a number up to the nearest odd integer.**

Syntax:

=ODD (number)

Parameter list:

number - The number to round up to an odd integer.

Points to note.

Negative numbers are rounded "up", away from zero, so they will become more negative.
If the number is nonnumeric, ODD returns the #VALUE! error value.

Examples:

=ODD(3.5)	Rounds 3.5 up to the nearest odd integer 5.
=ODD(5)	Rounds 5 up to the nearest odd integer 5.
=ODD(4)	Rounds 4 up to the nearest odd integer 5.
=ODD(-3)	Rounds -3 up to the nearest odd integer -3.
=ODD(-4)	Rounds -4 up (away from 0) to the nearest odd integer -5.

8.18. PI

This function returns the **mathematical constant pi, 3.14159265358979.**

Syntax:

=PI ()

There is no arguments for PI.

Examples:

=PI() Returns pi 3.141592654.

=PI()/ 3 Returns pi divided by 3 gives 1.047197551.
=PI()*(A1^2) Area of a circle with the radius described in A1 (cell A1 value is 4) gives 50.26548246.

8.19. POWER

This function returns the result of a **number raised to a power**.

Syntax:

POWER(number, power)

Parameter list:

number - the base number. It can be any real number.
power - the exponent to which the base number is raised.

Examples:

=POWER(4,2)   4 squared means 4 x 4 will get 16.
=POWER(4,3)   means 4 x 4 x 4 will get 64.
=POWER(58.3,4.1) 58.3 raised to the power of 4.1 will get 17347666.9011973.
=POWER(4,6/5) 4 raised to the power of 6/5 will get 5.27803164309158.

8.20. PRODUCT

This function multiplies all the numbers given as arguments and returns the product. = Product (A1,A2) will multiply the two numbers in the cell A1 and A2.

Syntax:

PRODUCT(number1, [number2], ...)

Parameter list:

number1 - the first number or range that you want to multiply.
number2 [optional]. additional numbers or ranges that you want to multiply, up to a maximum of 255 arguments.

Points to note.

If an argument is an array or reference, only numbers in the array or reference are multiplied. Empty cells, logical values, and text in the array or reference are ignored.

Examples:

=PRODUCT (A1:A5) will multiply the values in A1 to A5 and return the PRODUCT. It is like multiplying A1 x A2 X A3 X A4 X A5.

8.21. QUOTIENT

This function **returns the integer portion of a division and discard the reminder**. For Example =QUOTIENT(5, 2) we will get 2 as the answer as 2 x 2 is four and the remainder 1 is discarded. =QUOTIENT(7, 2) will give the answer 3 as 2 x 3 is 6 and the balance 1 is discarded.

Syntax:

QUOTIENT(numerator, denominator)

Points to note.

numerator – the dividend.
denominator - the divisor.

If either argument is nonnumeric, QUOTIENT returns the #VALUE! error value.

Examples:

=QUOTIENT(7, 2)	Integer portion of 7/2 is 3.
=QUOTIENT(9, 2)	Integer portion of 9/2 is 4.
=QUOTIENT(5.5, 4.1)	Integer portion of 4.5/3.1 is 1.
=QUOTIENT(-13, 4)	Integer portion of -10/3 is -3.

8.22. RAND

This function will return a **random number between 0 and 1** and there is no argument for this function. Each time the page is refreshed or the function is used it will generate different values.

Syntax:

RAND()

If you don't want the random numbers to be generated you have to copy the cell and paste it as values using paste special.

Or else if you want get a random number that doesn't change when the worksheet is calculated, enter =RAND() in the formulas bar and then press F9 to convert the formula into its result.

Also to generate a set of random numbers in multiple cells, select the cells, enter RAND() and press Control + enter.

To generate a random number between a and b, use this formula: RAND() * (b - a) + a.

8.23. RANDBETWEEN

This function will return a random integer between two values you supply. For example, =RANDBETWEEN(1,50) might generate the number 38 RANDBETWEEN calculates a new value each time the worksheet is calculated.

Syntax:

=RANDBETWEEN (bottom, top)

Parameter list:

bottom - an integer representing the lower value of the range.
top - an integer representing the lower value of the range.

To stop random numbers from being updated, copy the cells that contain RANDBETWEEN and paste it as values using paste special. To generate a set of random integers in multiple cells, select the cells, enter the RANDBETWEEN function, and press Control + Enter.

To get a random number that doesn't change when the worksheet is calculated, enter RANDBETWEEN in the formulas bar and then press F9 to convert the formula into its result.

8.24. ROMAN

This function converts an **Arabic numeral to Roman**, as text.

Syntax:

ROMAN(number, [form])

Parameter list:

number - the Arabic numeral you want converted.
form - a number specifying the type of roman numeral you want. The roman numeral style ranges from Classic to Simplified, becoming more concise as the value of form increases.

Form	Type
0 or omitted	Classic.
1	More concise. See example below.
2	More concise. See example below.
3	More concise. See example below.
4	Simplified.
TRUE	Classic.
FALSE	Simplified.

Points to note.

If number is negative, the #VALUE! error value is returned.
If number is greater than 3999, the #VALUE! error value is returned.

Examples:

=ROMAN(599,0)	Classic roman numeral style for 599 which is DXCIX.
=ROMAN(599,1)	More concise version for 599 which is DVCIV.

=ROMAN(599,2)	More concise version for 599 which is DIC.
=ROMAN(599,3)	More concise version for 599 which is DIC.
=ROMAN(599,4)	Simplified version for 599 which is DIC.

8.25. ROUND

This function **rounds a number to a given number of digits**. =ROUND(45.2564,2) will give you 45.25, rounded to two decimal places.

Syntax:

=ROUND (number, num_digits)

Parameter list:

number - the number to round.
num_digits - the number of digits to which number should be rounded.

Points to note.

Round works by rounding numbers 1-4 down, and rounding numbers 5-9 up.
The ROUND function rounds numbers to a specified level of precision. It can round to the right or left of the decimal point.
If num_digits > 0, number is rounded to the specified number of decimal places to the right of the decimal point.
If num_digits < 0, number is rounded to the left of the decimal point (i.e. to the nearest 10, 100, 1000, etc.).
If num_digits = 0, number is rounded to the nearest integer.

Examples:

=ROUND(32.85, 1)	Rounds 32.85 to one decimal place as 32.9.
=ROUND(4.859, 1)	Rounds 4.859 to one decimal place as 4.9.
=ROUND(-8.965, 2)	Rounds -8.965 to two decimal places as -8.97.
=ROUND(31.5, -1)	Rounds 31.5 to one decimal place to the left of the decimal point to 30.
=ROUND(546.3,-3)	Rounds 546.3 to three decimal place to the left of the decimal point to 1000.
=ROUND(1.14,-1)	Rounds 1.14 to the nearest multiple of 10 , which is 0.
=ROUND(-60.55,-2)	Rounds -60.55 to the nearest multiple of 100 which is -100.

8.26. ROUNDDOWN

This function **rounds a number down to a given number of digits** towards zero.

Syntax:

=ROUNDDOWN (number, num_digits)

Parameter list:

number - the number to round down.
num_digits - the number of digits to which number should be rounded down.

The ROUNDDOWN function works like the ROUND function except that when rounding, the ROUNDDOWN function will always round the numbers 1-9 down.

The ROUNDDOWN function can round either to the left or right of the decimal point.
If num_digits > 0, number is rounded down to the specified number of decimal places to the right of the decimal point.
If num_digits < 0, number is rounded down to the left of the decimal point (i.e. to the nearest 10, 100, 1000, etc.).
If num_digits = 0, number is rounded down to the nearest integer.

Examples:

=ROUNDDOWN(4.2,0)   Rounds 4.2 down to zero decimal places to 4.
=ROUNDDOWN(89.9,0) Rounds 89.9 down to zero decimal places to 89.
=ROUNDDOWN(9.23687,3) Rounds 9.23687 down to three decimal places to 9.236.
=ROUNDDOWN(-9.23687,1) Rounds -9.23687 down to one decimal place to -9.2.
=ROUNDDOWN(98546.356994,-2) Rounds 98546.356994 down to 2 decimal places to the left of the decimal point to 98500.

8.27. ROUNDUP

This function **rounds a number up to a given number of digits**, away from zero.

Syntax:

=ROUNDUP (number, num_digits)

Parameter list:

number - the number to round up.
num_digits - the number of digits to which number should be rounded up.

Usage notes:

The ROUNDUP function works like the ROUND function except that when rounding, the ROUNDUP function will always round the numbers 1-9 up.

ROUNDUP can round either to the left or right of the decimal point.
If num_digits > 0, number is rounded up to the specified number of decimal places to the right of the decimal point.
If num_digits < 0, number is rounded up to the left of the decimal point (i.e. to the nearest 10, 100, 1000, etc.).
If num_digits = 0, number is rounded up to the nearest integer.

Examples:

=ROUNDUP(4.2,0) Rounds 4.2 up to zero decimal places to 5.
=ROUNDUP(66.9,0) Rounds 66.9 up to zero decimal places to 67.
=ROUNDUP(8.56987, 3) Rounds 8.56987 up to three decimal places to 8.57.
=ROUNDUP(-9.47952, 1) Rounds -9.47952 up to one decimal place to -9.5.
=ROUNDUP(84555.92654, -2) Rounds 84555.92654 up to 2 decimal places to the left of the decimal point to 84600.

8.28. SQRT

This function will return the **positive square root of a number.**

Syntax:

=SQRT (number)

Parameter list:

number - the number to get the square root of.

	A	B	C
1	Numbers	Square Root	
2	-15	#NUM!	=SQRT(A2)
3	25	5	=SQRT(A3)
4	16	4	=SQRT(A4)
5	15.54	3.942080669	=SQRT(A5)

Points to note.

The SQRT function will return a #NUM error when asked to take the square root of a negative number.

8.29. SUBTOTAL

This function will create a subtotal in a list or database.

Syntax:

SUBTOTAL(function_num,ref1,[ref2],...)

Parameter list:

function_num - a number that specifies which function to use in calculating subtotals within a list. Details are provided below.
ref1 - a named range or cell reference to subtotal.
ref2 - [optional] a named range or cell reference to subtotal.

Function_num details.

Function_num (includes hidden	Function_num (ignores hidden	Function name

values)	values)	
1	101	AVERAGE
2	102	COUNT
3	103	COUNTA
4	104	MAX
5	105	MIN
6	106	PRODUCT
7	107	STDEV
8	108	STDEVP
9	109	SUM
10	110	VAR
11	111	VARP

Points to note.

Function_num constants from 1 to 11, the SUBTOTAL function includes the values of rows hidden. For the function_num constants from 101 to 111, the SUBTOTAL function ignores values of rows hidden.

The SUBTOTAL function ignores any rows that are not included in the result of a filter, no matter which function_num value you use. So if you have filtered any values and want to find the SUM or AVERAGE of the filtered values you should use this function as it does not consider the unfiltered values. For example, cell A1 has the value 10, A2 has 20 and A3 has 30 and if you filter out the value 10 and use the SUM formula you will get the total as 60 but if you use the formula SUBTOTAL to find out the total then you will get only filtered values total which is 50.

The SUBTOTAL function is designed for columns of data, or vertical ranges.

Check the example file exceltovba.com-SUBTOTAL.xlsx

	A	B
1	Values	
2	130	
3	20	
4	140	
5	33	
6		
7	Result	SUBTOTAL(function_num,ref1,[ref2],...)
8	323	=SUBTOTAL(9,A2:A5)
9	80.75	=SUBTOTAL(1,A2:A5)

In this example first we are calculating the sum of the subtotal of the cells A2:A5, using 9 as the first argument. 9 is for finding the sum including any hidden rows.

Second we are calculating the average of the subtotal of the cells A2:A5, using 1 as the first argument. 1 is used for finding the average including any hidden rows.

8.30. SUM

Sum formula is one of the easiest and the most used formula in Excel. It is used to **find the Sum of a cell ranges** or ranges.

Syntax:

SUM(number1,[number2],...)

Parameter list:

number1 - first number you want to add. The number can be like 5, a cell reference like A6, or a cell range like A2:A8.

number2 – [Optional] - the second number you want to add. You can specify up to 255 additional numbers in this way.

You can use the formula as shown below.

1. =SUM(25,65,78)
2. =SUM(A1,A2,A3) assuming 25,65,78 in the cells A1, A2, A3.
3. =SUM(A1:A3) assuming 25,65,78 in the cells A1, A2, A3.

In all these cases you will get 168 as the answer. But the easiest way to find the answer is the third one, SUM(A1:A3).

If you want to find the sum of the cells from A1 to A20000, you can just type =SUM(A1:A20000) in any of the cells.

Example 1:

Check the example file exceltovba.com-SUM.xlsx sheet name One.

E12	▾ : × ✓ fx		
	A	B	C
1	**Name**	**Marks**	
2	John	65	
3	Jenu	85	
4	Melvin	45	
5	Rambo	66	
6	Kevin	46	
7	Roy	80	
8			
9	Total marks	387	=SUM(B2,B3,B4,B5,B6,B7)
10	Total Marks of John and Jenu	150	=SUM(B2:B3)
11	Total Marks of John, Jenu, Rambo and Kevin	262	=SUM(B2:B3,B5:B6)

In this example you can see the total marks calculated in the cell B9 using the formula =SUM(B2,B3,B4,B5,B6,B7) as well the total marks calculated for the first two students using the formula =SUM(B2:B3) in the cell B10.

Also you can see the total marks for some of the students in-between using the formula =SUM(B2:B3,B5:B6) in the cell B11.

You can use the keyboard shortcut **ALT + =** to get the sum of a range very fast.

Example 2: Using Sum to find out the running total.

Please select the sheet name Two and in that you can see we are calculating the running total of the column B in column C.

Enter the SUM formula like this =SUM($B$2:B2) in the C2 cell. In the first cell reference we are putting one dollar sign each before the column and row number to lock the cell so when you copy the cell down it will still find the SUM from the cell B2 to the cell till you copy the formula.

F5		:	×	✓	fx	

	A	B	C	D	E	
1	Month	Sales	Running total			
2	Jan-15	50	50	=SUM($B$2:B2)		
3	Feb-15	55	105	=SUM($B$2:B3)		
4	Mar-15	68	173	=SUM($B$2:B4)		
5	Apr-15	78	251	=SUM($B$2:B5)		[
6	May-15	19	270	=SUM($B$2:B6)		
7	Jun-15	28	298	=SUM($B$2:B7)		
8	Jul-15		298	=SUM($B$2:B8)		
9	Aug-15		298	=SUM($B$2:B9)		
10	Sep-15		298	=SUM($B$2:B10)		
11	Oct-15		298	=SUM($B$2:B11)		
12	Nov-15		298	=SUM($B$2:B12)		
13	Dec-15		298	=SUM($B$2:B13)		

Example 3: Find out total sales for three months using VLOOKUP and SUM.

Check the example file exceltovba.com-SUM.xlsx sheet name Three.

	A	B	C	D	E	F
1	Products	Jan-15	Feb-15	Mar-15		
2	Wiper	46	12	32		
3	Headlight	30	38	38		
4	Break pads	35	99	81		
5	Oil Filter	99	95	16		
6	Silencer	61	68	35		
7						
8	Products	Total Sales				
9	Wiper	90	{=SUM(VLOOKUP(A10,$A$2:$D$6,{2,3,4},0))}			
10	Headlight	106	{=SUM(VLOOKUP(A11,$A$2:$D$6,{2,3,4},0))}			
11	Chain	#N/A	{=SUM(VLOOKUP(A12,$A$2:$D$6,{2,3,4},0))}			
12	Oil Filter	210	{=SUM(VLOOKUP(A13,$A$2:$D$6,{2,3,4},0))}			
13	Silencer	164	{=SUM(VLOOKUP(A14,$A$2:$D$6,{2,3,4},0))}			

In this example file we are clubbing VLOOKUP with SUM to find out the total sales for three months. First we will check the Product name matches and then we will sum all the sales figures from Jan to Mar 2015.

We will first enter the formula like this =SUM(VLOOKUP(A10,$A$2:$D$6,{2,3,4},0)) in B9, inside the sum we have put the VLOOKUP formula and the third parameter we have given the values as array constants like this {2,3,4} so that the VLOOKUP will get the values from the three columns 2, 3 and 4 which is Jan ,Feb and March against the product you specify and make an array in the memory and SUM will total the values.

Since this is an array formula instead of pressing Enter we should press Ctrl + Shift + Enter so that the formula will be changed to {=SUM(VLOOKUP(A10,$A$2:$D$6,{2,3,4},0))} with curly brackets at beginning and end. It is important you should press Ctrl + Shift + Enter otherwise it will get only sum of first value only and don't enter the Curly brackets manually Excel will put the brackets when you press Ctrl + Shift + Enter.

Since VLOOKUP has to compare according to the array value (here there are three values in each comparison {2,3,4}) you supplied it is advisable not to use it in big tables as it will slow down the Excel considerably. Instead of VLOOKUP you can use INDEX and MATCH functions.

Example 4: Sum using names instead of cell references.

Please open the sheet name Four and here we are finding out the Total sales by adding the sales for Jan, Feb and Mar. First we are naming the entire column A to Jan and for that we will select the entire Column and then change the cell reference shown in the Name box from A1 to Jan. Like that we will name the same for B column and C column to Feb and Mar.

Once you have done that you can call the cell reference from A column by Jan and B column to Feb and C column to Mar.

Enter =Jan+Feb+Mar in the E2 column and you will get the Sum of all months. The beauty of naming the cell or cells is you can call the Jan sales figure from the Z column or AM column, you don't have to remember the Feb sales column is in B or C.

And second thing is you will get the name of cells in the Auto complete list of named cells when you type the formula and you can press the TAB button to complete the cell reference.

The downside is if you delete the named ranges then you will get error because the SUM function will be looking for the names instead of the cell reference.

Example 5: Using OFFSET and SUM to calculate the SUM of ranges.

Go to sheet name Five, here we are clubbing together SUM and OFFSET to find the sales.

	A	B	C	D	E	F	G
1	Jan	Feb	Mar	Apr	May	June	July
2	65	59	85	95	73	65	92
3	55	56	64	86	67	65	86
4	81	83	86	97	51	57	88
5	86	72	67	54	83	85	87
6	68	79	74	59	86	75	61
7	95	67	92	88	94	75	56
8	99	57	58	90	91	52	94
9							
10	Jan Total sales			549	=SUM(A2:OFFSET(A2,7,0))		
11	Feb Total sales			473	=SUM(B2:OFFSET(B2,7,0))		
12	Total sales			3700	=SUM(A2:OFFSET(A2,7,6))		
13					Enter		
14	Enter Start month no.			0	0 for Jan		
15	Enter End Month no.			1	1 for Feb		
16	Result			1022	2 of Mar		
17	=SUM(OFFSET(A2,0,D14):OFFSET				3 for April		
18	(A2,7,D15))				4 for May		
19					5 for June		
20					6 for July		

First we are finding out the total sale for Jan, for that we have entered the formula =SUM(A2:OFFSET(A2,7,0)). Offset formula will give the cell reference A8 to second parameter of SUM function and will return the Sum from A2 to A8. Likewise we are calculating the Sum of Feb.

And lastly we are calculating the Total sales using the formula =SUM(OFFSET(A2,0,D14):OFFSET(A2,7,D15)) for the months according to the month number you are entering to the cell references D14 and D15 ,0 for Jan, 1 for Feb like that till 6 for July. Start month no. and End month no. are column number of OFFSET function from cell A2.

Example 6:

Go to sheet name Six, there we have include sales person also apart from the Start month and End month.

	A	B	C	D	E	F	G	H
1	Name	Jan	Feb	Mar	Apr	May	June	July
2	John	65	59	85	95	73	65	92
3	Jenu	55	56	64	86	67	65	86
4	Melvin	81	83	86	97	51	57	88
5	Rambo	86	72	67	54	83	85	87
6	Kevin	68	79	74	59	86	75	61
7	Roy	95	67	92	88	94	75	56
8	Mary	99	57	58	90	91	52	94
9								
10	Enter Start month no.			0	Enter		Enter	
11	Enter End Month no.			6	0 for Jan		0 for John	
12	Enter Sales Person No.			6	1 for Feb		1 for Jenu	
13					2 of Mar		2 of Melvin	
14	Result			541	3 for April		3 for Rambo	
15	=SUM(OFFSET(B2,D12,D10):OFFSET				4 for May		4 for Kevin	
16	(B2,D12,D11))				5 for June		5 for Roy	
17					6 for July		6 for Mary	

8.31. SUMIF

This function is used to **sum numbers in a range that meet the criteria** you supplied. For example if you want to sum only the values in a cell range which is greater than 20, you can set the formula like this =SUMIF(A2:A55,">20")

Syntax:

=SUMIF (range, criteria, [sum_range])

Parameter list:

range - the range of cells that you want to apply the criteria against ,must be numbers or names, arrays, or references that contain numbers. Blank and text values are ignored.
criteria - the criteria used to determine which cells to add.
sum_range - [optional] the cells to add together. If sum_range is omitted, the cells in range are added together instead.

Check the example file exceltovba.com-SUMIF.xlsx

	A	B	C	D	E	F	G	H
1	Zone	Sales						
2	South	47						
3	East	80		South	260	=SUMIF(A2:A16,D3,B2:B16)		
4	West	82		East	242	=SUMIF(A2:A16,D4,B2:B16)		
5	West	31		West	193	=SUMIF(A2:A16,D5,B2:B16)		
6	South	26		North	168	=SUMIF(A2:A16,D6,B2:B16)		
7	North	45	Greater than 80		260	=SUMIF(B2:B16,">80")		
8	East	25						
9	South	80						
10	North	42						
11	East	97						
12	South	74						
13	North	81						
14	East	40						
15	South	33						
16	West	80						

In the example file first we are finding out the total sale in the zone South. For that first we will select all the cell range which contains the zone name (Cell range A2:A16) and second parameter we are entering the zone name Itself whlch Is South. You can enter the name directly in double quotes like this "South" or you can point to a cell containing the text South.

Third parameter we are supplying the cell range from which we want to get the Sum of the sales of South zone (Cell range B2:B16).

Also you can use the formula directly to the cell range like this =SUMIF(B2:B16,">80") to get the sum of the values whlch Is greater than 80.

Points to note.

Any text or logical or mathematical symbols must be enclosed in double quotation marks (").

If the criteria is numeric double quotation marks are not required.

The wildcard characters ? and * can be used in criteria. A question mark matches any one character and an asterisk matches any sequence of characters. If you want to find an actual question mark or asterisk, type a tilde (~) preceding the character like this ~?, ~*.

8.32. SUMIFS

This function will **add the cells that match multiple criteria**.

Syntax:

=SUMIFS (sum_range, range1, criteria1, [range2], [criteria2], ...)

Parameter list:

sum_range - The range to be added.
range1 - The first range to evaulate.
criteria1 - The criteria to use on range1.
range2 - [optional] the second range to evaluate.
criteria2 - [optional] the criteria to use on range2.

Unlike SUMIF function SUMIFS function can check more than one set of criteria. First parameter is the one which will be summed. The criteria is to be given as pairs and only the first pair is compulsory and rest of the pairs are optional. You can enter up to 127 range/criteria pairs.

Points to note.

Using wildcard characters like the question mark (?) and asterisk (*) in criteria1 and criteria2 can help you find matches that are similar but not exact.

A question mark matches any single character. An asterisk matches any sequence of characters. If you want to find an actual question mark or asterisk, type a tilde (~) in front of the question mark.

Each additional range must have the same number of rows and columns as the sum_range.

Non-numeric criteria needs to be enclosed in double quotes but numeric criteria does not. For example: 100, "100", ">32", "jim", or A1 (where A1 contains a number).

Check the example file exceltovba.com-SUMIFS.xlsx

	A	B	C	D	E	F	G	H
1	Zone	Sales person	Month	Sales				
2	East	Joseph	Jan	553				
3	West	Maria	Feb	954				
4	North	John	Mar	725				
5	South	Melvin	April	817				
6	West	Jeswin	Feb	169				
7	North	Saibu	Mar	381				
8	South	Rony	April	597				
9	East	Vijay	Feb	717				
10	West	Monica	Mar	720				
11	North	George	Jan	202				
12	South	Denis	Feb	357				
13	East	Dora	Mar	907				
14	West	Symenthy	Jan	135				
15								
16	Total Sales East Zone for Jan			553	=SUMIFS(D2:D14,A2:A14,A2,C2:C14,C2)			
17	Total Sales West Zone for Feb			1123	=SUMIFS(D2:D14,A2:A14,A3,C2:C14,C3)			
18	Total Sales North Zone for Mar			1106	=SUMIFS(D2:D14,A2:A14,A4,C2:C14,C4)			
19	Total Sales South Zone for April			1414	=SUMIFS(D2:D14,A2:A14,A5,C2:C14,C5)			

In this example first we are checking the total sales done for East zone for the month of Jan. For that we are using the formula **=SUMIFS(D2:D14,A2:A14,A2,C2:C14,C2).** First parameter we are giving the cell range from which we should get the Sum and second parameter we are providing the cell range from which should pick the zone East, third parameter we have to give the criteria which has to be searched in the second parameter "East", since this can be hardcoded or we can give as a cell reference and here we have provided as cell reference.

Again we are giving the second range and the criteria as fourth and fifth parameters to pick the Jan sales from months.

Likewise we have done for West, North and South.

8.33. SUMPRODUCT

This function will **multiply the correspondent components in the given arrays and return the sum of the product**. For example =SUMPRODUCT(A1:A10,B1:B10) will multiply like this A1 x B1, A2 X B2, A3 X B3 and after multiplying will Sum the multiplied values.

Syntax:

=SUMPRODUCT (array1, [array2], ...)

Parameter list:

array1 - the first array or range to multiply, then add.
array2 - [optional] The second array or range to multiply, then add.

This function is more versatile than what we see. Since this function is using arrays we can use like the SUMIFS function.

Check the example file exceltovba.com-SUMPRODUCT.xlsx sheet1

	A	B	C	D	E	F	G
1	Name	Sales amount					
2	John	2500					
3	Vijay	6500					
4	John	5500					
5	Melvin	5000					
6	Vijay	3500					
7	Mary	4000					
8							
9	Total sales of Vijay		10000	=SUMPRODUCT(--(A2:A7="Vijay"),B2:B7)			
10	Total sales of John		8000	=SUMPRODUCT(--(A2:A7="John"),B2:B7)			

In this example file first we are finding the total sales done by Vijay. So when this formula is executed internally the array will look like this.

Array1 Array2

FALSE   2500
TRUE   6500
FALSE   5500
FALSE   5000
TRUE   3500
FALSE   4000

Since 2nd and 5th row has the name Vijay we will get the logical value TRUE for those two cases. Since we cannot multiply the logical value with the amount as Excel considers the logical value as 0 we can change the logical value to 1 and 0 for TRUE and FALSE using two negative signs after the first bracket.

So the two arrays will look like this when two negative signs are entered.

Array1   Array2 Product

0	*	2500	0
1	*	6500	6500
0	*	5500	0
0	*	5000	0
1	*	3500	3500
0	*	4000	0

As you can see this function will then make the total of the products like this 6500+3500 = 10000. The formula will look like this after entering the double negative values,

=SUMPRODUCT({0,1,0,0,1,0},{2500,6500,5500,5000,3500,4000})

8.34. TRUNC

This function **removes the fractional part** from the number to an integer.

Syntax::

TRUNC(number, [num_digits])

Parameter list:

number - the number to truncate.
num_digits – a number specifying the precision of the truncation. The default value for num_digits is 0 (zero).

check the example file exceltovba.com-TRUNC.xls

	A	B	C	D
1	Number	num-digits	Result	
2	8.2	0	8	=TRUNC(A2)
3	4.33	0	4	=TRUNC(A3,B3)
4	5.3333	0	5	=TRUNC(A4,B4)
5	-8.9	0	-8	=TRUNC(A5,B5)
6	0.4	0	0	=TRUNC(A6,B6)
7	8.2	0	8	=TRUNC(A7,B7)
8	8.23	1	8.2	=TRUNC(A8,B8)
9	4.3356	3	4.335	=TRUNC(A9,B9)
10	5.3333	0	5	=TRUNC(A10,B10)
11	-8.9	0	-8	=TRUNC(A11,B11)
12	0.4	0	0	=TRUNC(A12,B12)
13	12345.63	-1	12340	=TRUNC(A13,B13)
14	12345.63	-2	12300	=TRUNC(A14,B14)
15	12345.63	-3	12000	=TRUNC(A15,B15)

TRUNC and INT are similar functions. TRUNC removes the fractional part of the number. INT rounds numbers down to the nearest integer based on the value of the fractional part of the number. INT and TRUNC are different only when using negative numbers; TRUNC(-8.3) returns -8 but INT(-8.3) returns -9 because -9 is the lower number.

9. Statistical

9.1. AVERAGE

This formulas **calculates the average** of a given cell or cell range.

Syntax:

AVERAGE(number1, [number2], ...)

Parameter list:

number1 - the first number, cell reference, or range for which you want the average.
number2 [optional]. Additional numbers, cell references or ranges for which you want the average, up to a maximum of 255.

Examples:

=AVERAGE(25,65,78)
=AVERAGE(A1,A2,A3)
=AVERAGE(A1:A3)

In all these cases you will get 56 as the answer. But the easiest way to find the answer is the third one, AVERAGE (A1:A3). If you want to find the AVERAGE of the cells from A1 to A20000, you can just type = AVERAGE (A1:A20000) in any of the cells.

In the AVERAGE Excel sheet go to the sheet name one and see what the three ways in which sum formula is used.

	A	B	C
1	Name	Marks	
2	John	65	
3	Jenu	85	
4	Melvin	45	
5	Rambo	66	
6	Kevin	46	
7	Roy	80	
8			
9	Average marks	64.50	=AVERAGE(B2,B3,B4,B5,B6,B7)
10	Average Marks of John and Jenu	75	=AVERAGE(B2:B3)
11	Average Marks of John, Jenu, Rambo and Kevin	65.5	=AVERAGE(B2:B3,B5:B6)

In the sheet name two you can see the average marks calculated in the cell B9 using the formula = AVERAGE (B2,B3,B4,B5,B6,B7) as well the average marks calculated for the first two students using the formula = AVERAGE (B2:B3) in the cell B10.

Also you can see the average marks for some of the students in-between using the formula = AVERAGE (B2:B3,B5:B6) in the cell B11.

9.2. AVERAGEIF

This function returns the **average of all the cell in a range** that meets the condition.

Syntax:

AVERAGEIF(range, criteria, [average_range])

Parameter list:

range - one or more cells to average, including numbers or names, arrays, or references that contain numbers.
criteria - the criteria in the form of a number, expression, cell reference, or text that defines which cells are averaged.
average_range - [Optional]. the actual set of cells to average. If omitted, range is used.

Check the example file exceltovba.com-AVERAGEIF.xlsx

	A	B	C	D	E	F	G	H
1	Zone	Sales						
2	South	47				AVERAGEIF(range, criteria, [average_range]]		
3	East	80		South	52	=AVERAGEIF(A2:B16,D3,B2:B16)		
4	West	82		North	56	=AVERAGEIF(A2:B16,D6,B2:B16)		
5	West	31	Greater than 80		82	=AVERAGEIF(B2:B16,">50")		
6	South	26		South	52	=AVERAGEIF(A2:A16,D6,B2:B4)		
7	North	45		South	36.5	=AVERAGEIF(A2:A6,D7,B2:B16)		
8	East	25	Except south		60.3	=AVERAGEIF(A2:A16,"<>South",B2:B16)		
9	South	80						
10	North	42						
11	East	97						
12	South	74						
13	North	81						
14	East	40						
15	South	33						
16	West	80						

In this example first two entries we are calculating the average sales of South and North. Third we are calculating the average sales if the sales is greater than 80. Fourth we are again calculating the average of South zone but here you can see the range and average_range are different but still the average will be calculated on the range itself. Fifth one also we are calculating the average of South, even though we have selected the average_range fully average will be calculated on the range we have selected in the first parameter.

And the last one we are calculating the average of all the zones which is not South.

Points to note.

Cells in range that contain TRUE or FALSE are ignored.

If a cell in average_range is an empty cell, AVERAGEIF ignores it.
If range is a blank or text value, AVERAGEIF returns the #DIV0! error value.
If a cell in criteria is empty, AVERAGEIF treats it as a 0 value.
If no cells in the range meet the criteria, AVERAGEIF returns the #DIV/0! error value.

You can use the wildcard characters, question mark (?) (matches any single character) and asterisk (*) (matches any sequence of characters) . If you want to find an actual question mark or asterisk, type a tilde (~) before the character.

Average_range does not have to be the same size and shape as range. The actual cells that are averaged are determined by using the top, left cell in average_range as the beginning cell, and then including cells that correspond in size and shape to range

9.3. AVERAGEIFS

This function will **return the average of all cells that meet multiple criteria.**

Syntax:

AVERAGEIFS(average_range, criteria_range1, criteria1, [criteria_range2, criteria2], ...)

Parameter list:

average_range – cell or cells to average, including numbers or names, arrays, or references that contain numbers.
criteria_range1, criteria_range2, - criteria_range1 is mandatory and subsequent criteria_ranges are optional. You can supply up to 127 ranges with criteria.
criteria1, criteria2, ..- criteria1 is mandatory and subsequent criteria are optional. You can give up to 127 criteria. You can supply the criteria like 85, "89", ">78", "Banana", or A5.

Check the example file exceltovba.com-AVERAGEIFS.xlsx

	A	B	C	D	E	F	G	H
1	Price	Town	Bedrooms	Personal Chef				
2	240000	London	3	No				
3	182000	Paris	2	Yes				
4	360154	Paris	4	Yes				
5	337891	London	2	Yes				
6	440000	Paris	5	Yes				
7	385000	Paris	4	No				
8	AVERAGEIFS(average_range, criteria_range1, criteria1, [criteria_range2, criteria2], ...)							
9	Result							
10	400077	=AVERAGEIFS(A2:A6, B2:B6, "Paris", C2:C6, ">2",D2:D6, "Yes")						
11	240000	=AVERAGEIFS(A1:A6, B1:B6, "London", C1:C6, "<=3",D1:D6, "No")						

In this example first we are calculating the average price of hotel room from A column if the town is in Paris, having more than 3 Bedrooms and with a Personal Chef.
First parameter we should supply the column from which we want the average which is A2:A6.

Second and third parameter is the criteria range1 and criteria1 means the entire range having the town name and the town name to sort which is B2:B6 and Paris.

Fourth and the fifth parameter is the second criteria range (C2:C6) and the criteria (>2) , which is the number of bedrooms and the bedrooms more than 2.

Sixth and the seven parameter is the third criteria range (D2:D6) and the criteria (Yes), which means we are checking whether Personal Chef is there or not.

Second we are finding the average of the A column when the town is London and the bedroom is equal to or less than 3 and without a personal chef.

This function is same like using the filter function in Excel.

Points to note.

If average_range is a blank or text or no cells that meet all the criteria or cells in average_range cannot be translated into numbers you will get #DIV0! Error.

If a cell in a criteria range is empty, AVERAGEIFS treats it as a 0 value.

Cells in range contain TRUE will be treated as 1 and for FALSE will be treated as 0.

Unlike AVERAGEIF function, in AVERAGEIFS each criteria_range must be the same size and shape as sum_range.

You can use the wildcard characters, question mark (?) and asterisk (*), in criteria. A question mark matches any single character; an asterisk matches any sequence of characters. If you want to find an actual question mark or asterisk, type a tilde (~) before the character.

9.3. COUNT

This function will **count the numbers given in a cell reference** or range. For example, =COUNT(1, 8 "Orange") returns 2. And COUNT(A1:A100) will count the number of numeric values in the range A1:A100. Use COUNT to count numeric values only.

Syntax:

=COUNT (value1, [value2], ...)

Parameter list:

value1 - An item, cell reference, or range.
value2 - [optional] Up to 255 additional items, cell reference, or range.

Points to note.

Numbers, dates, or a text representation of numbers, a number enclosed in quotation marks, such as "1" are counted.

Logical values and text representations of numbers that you type directly into the list of arguments are counted.

Error values or text that cannot be translated into numbers are not counted.

If an argument is an array or reference, only numbers in that array or reference are counted.

If you want to count logical values, text, or error values, use the **COUNTA** function.

Check the example file exceltovba.com-COUNT.xlsx

	A	B
1	Values	
2	26-03-16	
3	25	
4	65.54	
5	TRUE	
6	#DIV/0!	
7		
8	COUNT (value1, [value2], ...)	
9	3	=COUNT(A2:A7)
10	0	=COUNT(A5:A7)
11	4	=COUNT(A2:A7,2)

In this example first we are counting the number of cells that contain numbers in cells A2 through A7, logical value and errors are avoided so we will get the count as 3.
Second we are counting the number of cells that contain numbers in cells A5 through A7. These cells have logical value and error value so count returns 0.
Third we are counting the number of cells that contain numbers in cells A2 through A7, and the value 2. A2 to A7 contains only three values and the value 2 is counted as the fourth one and we will get the answer as 4.

9.4. COUNTA

This function **counts the number of non-blank cells**. COUNTA function counts cells that contain numbers, text, logical values, error values, and empty text ("") except non-blank cells.

Syntax:

=COUNTA (value1, [value2], ...)

Parameter list:

value1 - an item, cell reference, or range.
value2 - [optional] an item, cell reference, or range. Up to a maximum of 255 arguments.

Check the example file exceltovba.com-COUNTA.xlsx

	A	B
1	**Values**	
2	26-03-16	
3	25	
4		
5	65.54	
6	TRUE	
7	#DIV/0!	
8		
9	COUNTA (value1, [value2], ...)	
10	5 =COUNTA(A2:A8)	

In this example you can see the COUNTA function counts all the values except blank cells.

9.5. COUNTBLANK

This function will **count cells that are blank**. For example, COUNTBLANK(A1:A100) will count the number of blank cells in the range A1:A100.

Syntax:

=COUNTBLANK (range)

Parameter list:

range - the range in which to count blank cells.

Points to note.

Cells with formulas that return "" (empty text) are also counted.
Cells with zero values are not counted.

9.6. COUNTIF

This function **count cells that match criteria** and returns a number representing cells counted.

Syntax:

=COUNTIF (range, criteria)

Parameter list:

range - the range of cells to count.
criteria - the criteria that controls which cells should be counted.

Check the example file exceltovba.com-COUNTIF.xlsx

	A	B	C	D	E	F	G
1	Zone	Sales					
2	South	47					
3	North	80				COUNTIF (range, criteria)	
4	East	82		South	6	=COUNTIF(A2:A16,D4)	
5	West	31		East	3	=COUNTIF(A2:B16,D5)	
6	South	26		West	2	=COUNTIF(A2:B16,D6)	
7	North	45		North	4	=COUNTIF(A2:B16,D7)	
8	South	25	Greater than 80		3	=COUNTIF(B2:B16,">80")	
9	South	80					
10	North	42					
11	East	97					
12	South	74					
13	North	81					
14	East	40					
15	South	33					
16	West	80					

In the example we are checking the count of the zone name South. For that we have supplied the first parameter as cell range A2:A16 and second parameter South itself. Likewise we are counting each zones.

And last we are counting how many sales has crossed above 80.

More examples:

=COUNTIF(A1:A100,200) // count cells equal to 200
=COUNTIF(A1:A100,">56") // count cells greater than 56
=COUNTIF(A1:A100,"sam") // count cells equal to "sam"
=COUNTIF(A1:A100,"<"&C1) // count cells less than value in C1

Points to note.

Range can contain numbers, arrays, a named range, or references that contain numbers. Blank and text values are ignored.

Any text must be enclosed in double quotation marks (").

If the criteria is numeric double quotation marks are not required.

The wildcard characters ? and * can be used in criteria. A question mark matches any one character and an asterisk matches any sequence of characters. If you want to find an actual question mark or asterisk, type a tilde (~) preceding the character like this ~?, ~*.

9.7. COUNTIFS

Syntax:

COUNTIFS(criteria_range1, criteria1, [criteria_range2, criteria2]...)

Parameter list:

criteria_range1 - the first range to evaluate.
criteria1 – the criteria for the criteria_range like 45, ">65", B4, "John", "<5/3/2011" ,or "96".
criteria_range2, criteria2, ...[Optional] additional ranges and their associated criteria, up to 127
range/criteria pairs are supported.

Example1:

Check the example file exceltovba.com-COUNTIFS.xlsx Sheet1

	A	B	C	D	E	F
1	Name	Jan	Feb	Mar		
2	John	Pass	Fail	Pass		
3	Sam	Pass	Pass	Pass		
4	Vijay	Fail	Fail	Pass		
5	Melvin	Fail	Pass	Fail		
6						
7	COUNTIFS(criteria_range1, criteria1, [criteria_range2, criteria2]...)					
8	Result					
9	7	=COUNTIFS(B2:D5,"Pass")				
10	5	=COUNTIFS(B2:D5,"Fail")				
11	1	=COUNTIFS(B2:B5,"pass",C2:C5,"pass",D2:D5,"pass")				

In this example first we are counting all the Students who have passed (indicated by the text Pass) in
Jan, Feb and Mar. Second we are counting how many have failed.

The last one we are counting how many students have passed In all the three months, for that first we
are giving the first criteria range (B2:B5) followed by the criteria 'Pass' followed by second criteria range
(C2:C5) and criteria 'Pass' and the last criteria range (D2:D5) and criteria 'Pass'. Since only one student
have passed the examInation in all the three months we will get the answer as 1.

Example2:

Check the example file exceltovba.com-COUNTIFS.xlsx Sheet2

	A	B	C	D	E	F	G
1	**Value**	**Dates**					
2	11	02-04-15					
3	12	03-04-15					
4	13	04-04-15					
5	14	05-04-15					
6	15	06-04-15					
7	16	07-04-15					
8							
9	**Result**	COUNTIFS(criteria_range1, criteria1, [criteria_range2, criteria2]...)					
10	4	=COUNTIFS(A2:A7,"<16",A2:A7,">11")					
11	3	=COUNTIFS(A2:A7, "<15",B2:B7,"<5/4/2015")					
12	2	=COUNTIFS(A2:A7, "<" & A6,B2:B7,"<" & B4)					

In this example first we are counting how many numbers are there between 11 and 16 in the cells A2 to A7.

Second we are counting how many rows have numbers that are less than 15 in cells A2 to A7 and have dates that are earlier than 5/04/2015 in cells B2 to B7.

Third we are using the cell reference instead of the constants in the criteria to find out how many rows have numbers that are less than the cell A6 which is 15 and have dates less than the cell B4 which is '04/04/2015', the answer will be 2.

Points to note.

Each additional range must have the same number of rows and columns as the criteria_range1.

You can use the wildcard characters, question mark (?) (matches any single character) and asterisk (*) (matches any sequence of characters) in the criteria. If you want to find an actual question mark or asterisk, type a tilde (~) before the character.

9.8. FREQUENCY

This function will count how often values occur within a range of values, and then returns a vertical array of numbers.

Syntax:

=FREQUENCY (data_array, bins_array)

Parameter list:

data_array - An array of values for which you want to get frequencies.
bins_array - An array of intervals ("bins") for grouping values.

Usage notes:

You can use Excel's FREQUENCY function to create a frequency distribution - a summary table that shows the frequency (count) of each value in a range. FREQUENCY counts how often values occur in a set of data. It returns a vertical array of numbers that represent frequencies.

Check the example file exceltovba.com-FREQUENCY.xlsx

	A	B	C
1	Scores	Bins	
2	49	55	
3	62	62	
4	89	75	
5	41		
6	97		
7	61		
8	55		
9	100		
10	71		
11			
12	Results	Formula	Description
13	3	{=FREQUENCY(A2:A10, B2:B4)}	No. of scores less than or equal to 55
14	2	{=FREQUENCY(A2:A10, B2:B4)}	No. of scores in the bin 56-62
15	1	{=FREQUENCY(A2:A10, B2:B4)}	No. of scores in the bin 63-75
16	3	{=FREQUENCY(A2:A10, B2:B4)}	No. of scores greater than or equal to 75

In this example we are checking the count of scores as per the Bins values. First you have to select four cells and enter the formula =FREQUENCY(A2:A10,B2:B4) and then press CTRL+Shift+Enter to change it to array formula. You can see all the cells has the same cell address and curly bracket to indicate it is an array formula.

You can see the results in the four cells from A13:A16. First this function is checking how many scores are at par or below the first bin value 55, then it checks how many scores in between 56 to 62 (above first bin value and up to second bin value) . Third it checks how many scores are occurring between 63 to 75 (above second bin value and upto third bin value) and lastly it checks how many scores are there above 75.

Points to note.

FREQUENCY always returns an array so it should be entered as an array formula by pressing CTRL+Shift+Enter after selecting all the cells.

The number of elements in the returned array is one more than the number of elements in bins_array. So if there are three Bins value then you must first select four cells and then enter the formula.

9.9. LARGE

This function returns **the kth largest value in a data set**. For example if you specify the k value as 1 it will return the largest value from the group and if you specify 2 it will return the second largest value from the group.

Syntax:

=LARGE (array, k)

Parameter list:

array - the data set from which you want to select the kth largest value.
k - integer that specifies the position from the largest value, i.e. the kth position.

Check the example file exceltovba.com-LARGE.xlsx

	A	B	C	D	E	F	G	H
J9				fx				
1	Values		Highest Value		900		=LARGE(A2:A6,1)	
2	100		2nd Highest Value		500		=LARGE(A2:A6,2)	
3	900		3rd Highest Value		450		=LARGE(A2:A6,3)	
4	300		4th Highest Value		300		=LARGE(A2:A6,4)	
5	500		5th Highest Value		100		=LARGE(A2:A6,5)	
6	450							

In the example file we are calculating the largest value from the group A2 to A6 using the formula =LARGE(A2:A6,1) and the largest value in the group is 900 and if you want the second highest you have to put the second parameter as 2 and you will get 500 and so on.

You can use this function to find out the first, second and third position in a Race or Exam.

9.10. MAX

This **function will return the largest value** from a cell range ignoring logical values and text.

Syntax:

= MAX(number1, [number2], ...)

Parameter list:

number1 – the number or numbers in cell range
number2 – [optional}. 1 to 255 numbers for which you want to find the maximum value.

Check the example file exceltovba.com-MAX.xlsx

	A	B	C
1		Values	Dates
2		25	14-03-16
3		85	14-01-16
4		15	14-01-15
5		65	14-05-16
6		75	25-03-15
7		25	29-10-15
8		95	08-01-15
9			
10	Max values	95	14-05-16
11		=MAX(B2:B8)	=MAX(C2:C8)

In this example file you can see we are finding the highest value in B column and the highest date in the C column.

In the Sheet2 we are finding the highest sales value for each month and also finding the sales person highest.

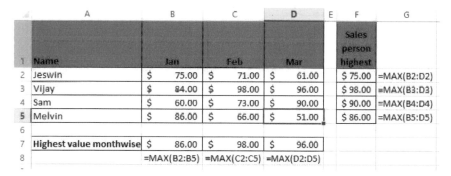

	A	B	C	D	E	F	G
1	Name	Jan	Feb	Mar		Sales person highest	
2	Jeswin	$ 75.00	$ 71.00	$ 61.00		$ 75.00	=MAX(B2:D2)
3	Vijay	$ 84.00	$ 98.00	$ 96.00		$ 98.00	=MAX(B3:D3)
4	Sam	$ 60.00	$ 73.00	$ 90.00		$ 90.00	=MAX(B4:D4)
5	Melvin	$ 86.00	$ 66.00	$ 51.00		$ 86.00	=MAX(B5:D5)
6							
7	Highest value monthwise	$ 86.00	$ 98.00	$ 96.00			
8		=MAX(B2:B5)	=MAX(C2:C5)	=MAX(D2:D5)			

9.11. MEDIAN

This function will **return the median of the numbers**. The median is the number in the middle of a set of numbers, half the numbers have values that are greater than the median, and half the numbers have values that are less than the median. For example, the median of 2, 3, 3, 5, 7, and 10 is 4.

Syntax:

=MEDIAN (number1, [number2], ...)

Parameter list:

number1 is mandatory and subsequent numbers are optional. 1 to 255 numbers for which you want the median.

	A	B	C	D
1	Values			
2	1			
3	3			
4	8	6	=MEDIAN(A2:A9)	
5	10	7.5	=MEDIAN(A2:A7)	
6	9			
7	7			
8	5			
9	2			

Points to note.

When the total number of supplied numbers is even, the median is calculated as the average of the two numbers in the middle.

9.12. MIN

This function will **return the smallest value** from set of cells.

Syntax:

=MIN (number1, [number2], ...)

number1 is mandatory, subsequent numbers are optional. 1 to 255 numbers for which you want to find the minimum value.

Check the example file exceltovba.com-MIN.xlsx

	A	B	C
1	Values		
2	5		
3	3		
4	2		
5	4		
6	8		
7			
8	Smallest Value	2	=MIN(A2:A6)

In this example we are getting the smallest value from the group which is two.

9.13. MINA

This function returns the **minimum value in a list of arguments**, including **logical values and text**.

Syntax:

MINA(value1, [value2], ...)

Value1, value2, ... value1 is required, subsequent values are optional. 1 to 255 values for which you want to find the smallest value.

Points to note.

Arguments can be numbers; names, arrays, or references that contain numbers; text representations of numbers; or logical values, such as TRUE and FALSE, in a reference.
If an argument is an array or reference, only values in that array or reference are used. Empty cells and text values in the array or reference are ignored.
Logical values TRUE evaluate as 1 and FALSE evaluate as 0 (zero).
Arguments that are error values or text that cannot be translated into numbers cause errors.

If you do not want to include logical values and text representations of numbers in a reference as part of the calculation, use the MIN function.

This is the same like MIN function except it uses logical values and text representations of numbers in a reference as part of the calculation

9.14. SMALL

This function **returns the kth smallest value in a data set**. For example if you specify the k value as 1 it will return the lowest value from the group and if you specify 2 it will return the second lowest value from the group.

Syntax:

=SMALL (array, k)

Parameter list:

array - a range of cells from which to extract smallest values.
k - an integer that specifies the position of the smallest value.

Check the example file exceltovba.com-SMALL.xlsx

E3		▼	:	×	✓	fx	=SMALL(A2:A6,3)

	A	B	C	D	E	F	G	H
1	Values		Smallest Value		100		=SMALL(A2:A6,1)
2	100		2nd Highest Value		300		=SMALL(A2:A6,2)
3	900		3rd Highest Value		450		=SMALL(A2:A6,3)
4	300		4th Highest Value		500		=SMALL(A2:A6,4)
5	500		5th Highest Value		900		=SMALL(A2:A6,5)
6	450						

In the example file we are calculating the smallest value from the group A2 to A6 using the formula =SMALL(A2:A6,1) and the smallest value in the group is 100 and if you want the second highest you have to put the second parameter as 2 and you will get 300 and so on.

10. Text

10.1. CHAR

This function coverts a **normal number to the character** it represents in the ANSI character set.

Syntax:

=CHAR (number)

Parameter list:

number - A number between 1 and 255.

No.	Char value	No.	Char value	No.	Char value	No.	Char value	No.	Char value	No.	Char value	No.	Char value	No.	Char value	No.	Char value	No.	Char value	No.	Char value
1		26	→	51	3	76	L	101	e	126	~	151	—	176	°	201	É	226	â	251	û
2	¬	27	←	52	4	77	M	102	f	127	□	152	˜	177	±	202	Ê	227	ã	252	ü
3	L	28		53	5	78	N	103	g	128	€	153	™	178	²	203	Ë	228	ä	253	ý
4	⌐	29		54	6	79	O	104	h	129		154	š	179	³	204	Ì	229	å	254	þ
5			30		55	7	80	P	105	i	130	,	155	›	180	´	205	Í	230	æ	255	ÿ
6	─	31		56	8	81	Q	106	j	131	ƒ	156	œ	181	µ	206	Î	231	ç		
7	•	32	•	57	9	82	R	107	k	132	„	157		182	¶	207	Ï	232	è		
8	◘	33	!	58	:	83	S	108	l	133	…	158	ž	183	·	208	Ð	233	é		
9		34	"	59	;	84	T	109	m	134	†	159	Ÿ	184	¸	209	Ñ	234	ê		
10		35	#	60	<	85	U	110	n	135	‡	160		185	¹	210	Ò	235	ë		
11	♪	36	$	61	=	86	V	111	o	136	ˆ	161	¡	186	º	211	Ó	236	ì		
12	♀	37	%	62	>	87	W	112	p	137	‰	162	¢	187	»	212	Ô	237	í		
13		38	&	63	?	88	X	113	q	138	Š	163	£	188	¼	213	Õ	238	î		
14	♫	39	'	64	@	89	Y	114	r	139	‹	164	¤	189	½	214	Ö	239	ï		
15	☼	40	(	65	A	90	Z	115	s	140	Œ	165	¥	190	¾	215	×	240	ð		
16	+	41	)	66	B	91	[	116	t	141		166	¦	191	¿	216	Ø	241	ñ		
17	◄	42	*	67	C	92	\	117	u	142	Ž	167	§	192	À	217	Ù	242	ò		
18	↕	43	+	68	D	93	]	118	v	143		168	¨	193	Á	218	Ú	243	ó		
19	‖	44	.	69	E	94	^	119	w	144		169	©	194	Ã	219	Û	244	ô		

CHAR can be useful when you want to specify characters in formulas or functions that are awkward or impossible to type directly. For example, you can use CHAR(10) to add a line break in a formula on Windows, and CHAR(13) to add a line break on the Mac.

10.2. CLEAN

This function **removes any non-printable characters from text**. Sometimes if you import data from other databases it may contain non-printable characters.

Syntax:

=CLEAN (text)

Parameter list:

text - the text to clean.

Note: The CLEAN function removes the first 32 (non-printable) characters in the 7-bit ASCII code (values 0 through 31) from text. Also in Unicode contains other nonprinting characters (values 127, 129, 141, 143, 144, and 157).

For example if the A2 cell has this formula =CHAR(9)&"Monthly report"&CHAR(10) there will be leading and trailing non-printable characters. So to remove that you can use the CLEAN function like this, =CLEAN(A2). Before entering the CLEAN function just check the length of the cell A2 using LEN function it will be 16 whereas the actual length should be 14, additional 2 is the non-printable characters.

10.3. CODE

This function **returns the ANSI value of a single character** or the first character in a text. The ANSI character set used by Windows to identify each keyboard character by using a unique number. There are 255 character in ANSI set. For Example ANSI code for letter A is 65, ANSI code for letter a is 97, ANSI code for letter B is 66.

Syntax:

=CODE (text)

Parameter list:

text - the text for which you want a numeric code.

	H12	▼ : × ✓ fx	
	A	B	C
1	**Letter**	**ANSI code**	**Formula used**
2	A	65	=CODE(A2)
3	B	66	=CODE(A3)
4	C	67	=CODE(A4)
5	D	68	=CODE(A5)
6	E	69	=CODE(A6)
7	a	97	=CODE(A7)
8	b	98	=CODE(A8)
9	c	99	=CODE(A9)
10	d	100	=CODE(A10)
11	e	101	=CODE(A11)
12	Ali	65	=CODE(A12)
13	Donald	68	=CODE(A13)
14	Egg	69	=CODE(A14)

10.4. CONCATENATE

This **function joins several text items into one text item**. CONCATENATE function combines text from different cells into one cell. In the example file enter =CONCATENATE(A2,B2) in the cell C2 and you can see the combined text in C2.

You may have noticed that the first and last names don't have a space in between. That's because CONCATENATE will combine exactly what you tell it to combine, and nothing more. If you want punctuation, spaces, or any other details to appear in the cell, you'll need to tell CONCATENATE to include it.

To add a space, we can simply add another argument: " " (two double quotes around a space). Make sure the three arguments are separated by commas:

=CONCATENATE(A2," ",B2)

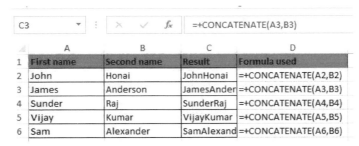

Like the above example you can add a coma or a word or any other character in between the names.

10.5. DOLLAR

This function **converts a number to text format** and applies a currency symbol.

Syntax:

=DOLLAR (number, [decimals])

Parameter list:

number - the number to convert.

decimals – [optional] - the number of digits to the right of the decimal point. Default is 2. If decimals is negative, number will be rounded to the left of the decimal point.

Usage notes:

The DOLLAR function converts a number to text using currency number format. The number format used is $#,##0.00_);($#,##0.00).

The TEXT function is a more flexible way to achieve the same result, since it can convert numbers to text in currency format and other number formats as well.

The currency symbol used is based on language settings of the computer.

Check the example file exceltovba.com-DOLLAR.xlsx

	A	B
1	Values	
2	1234.563	
3	-1234.57	
4	-0.189	
5	89.888	
6		
7	Result	DOLLAR (number, [decimals])
8	$1,234.56	=DOLLAR(A2, 2)
9	$1,200	=DOLLAR(A2, -2)
10	($1,200)	=DOLLAR(A3, -2)
11	($0.1890)	=DOLLAR(A4, 4)
12	$89.89	=DOLLAR(A5)

10.6. FIXED

This function **rounds the number to fixed number** of decimals and returns as text.

Syntax:

FIXED(number, [decimals], [no_commas])

Parameter list:

number - the number you want to round.

Decimals - the number of digits to the right of the decimal point, this is optional, default is 2.

no_commas – [optional] a logical TRUE or FALSE for including commas in the returned text. FALSE or omitted will have commas as usual.

Check the example file exceltovba.com-FIXED.xlsx

	A	B	C
1	**Data**		
2	56478.36589		
3	-56478.36589		
4	65.889		
5			
6	**Result**	**Description**	
7	56,478.4	Rounds the number in A2 one digit to the right of the decimal point.	=FIXED(A2, 1)
8	56,480	Rounds the number in A2 one digit to the left of the decimal point.	=FIXED(A2, -1)
9	-56480	Rounds the number in A3 one digit to the left of the decimal point, without commas (the TRUE argument).	=FIXED(A3, -1, TRUE)
10	65.89	Rounds the number in A4 two digits to the left of the decimal point.	=FIXED(A4)

10.7. LEFT

This function **returns the leftmost characters from a text** value based on the number of characters you specify.

Syntax:

=LEFT (text, [num_chars])

Parameter list:

text - the text from which to extract characters.
num_chars - [optional] the number of characters to extract, starting on the left side of text. Default = 1.

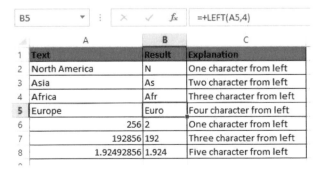

B5					f_x	=+LEFT(A5,4)

	A	B	C
1	**Text**	**Result**	**Explanation**
2	North America	N	One character from left
3	Asia	As	Two character from left
4	Africa	Afr	Three character from left
5	Europe	Euro	Four character from left
6	256	2	One character from left
7	192856	192	Three character from left
8	1.92492856	1.924	Five character from left

LEFT will extract digits from numbers as well.

10.8. LEN

This function **returns the number of characters** in a text string.

Syntax:

=LEN (text)

Parameter list:

text - The text for which to calculate length.

Check the example file exceltovba.com-LEN.xlsx

	A	B	C
1	Data	Result	
2	This	4	=LEN(A2)
3	How are you?	12	=LEN(A3)
4	Fine	4	=LEN(A4)
5	Joseph	6	=LEN(A5)
6	Merin James	11	=LEN(A6)
7	This	5	=LEN(A7)

In this example we are checking the length of each text using the Len function and you can see the length of the last word 'This' is shown as 5 whereas there are only four characters in the word 'This'. This is because there is a single space character after the character 's'. If you want to remove the excess space you can use the TRIM function.

10.9. LOWER

This function **converts text to lowercase**.

Syntax:

= LOWER(text)

Parameter list:

text - the text in a worksheet cell to be changed.

The text argument can be

a cell reference like this =LOWER(A1)
a word or words enclosed in quotation marks like this =LOWER("THIS IS FUN")
a formula that outputs text like this =LOWER(CONCATENATE(A4,A5,A6)), will merge all the data in the cell A4, A5 and A6 and change the case to lower.

Check the example file exceltovba.com-LOWER.xls

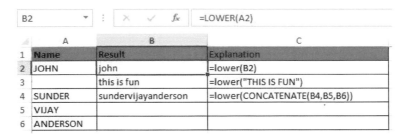

	A	B	C
1	**Name**	**Result**	Explanation
2	JOHN	john	=lower(B2)
3		this is fun	=lower("THIS IS FUN")
4	SUNDER	sundervijayanderson	=lower(CONCATENATE(B4,B5,B6))
5	VIJAY		
6	ANDERSON		

10.10. MID

This function **returns a specific number of characters** from a text string, starting at the position you specify.

Syntax:

=MID (text, start_num, num_chars)

Parameter list:

text - the text to extract from.
start_num - the location of the first character to extract.
num_chars - the number of characters to extract.

Check the example file exceltovba.com-MID.xls

	A	B	C
1	**Name**	**Result**	
2	john	oh	=MID(A2,2,2)
3	james anderson	ames	=MID(A3,2,5)
4	This is fun	This	=MID(A4,1,4)
5	vijay	jay	=MID(A5,3,3)
6	I love you too	love	=MID(A6,3,5)

10.11. PROPER

This function **capitalizes the first letter in each word** of a text value. As you can see in example given below the first letter of the word is capitalized.

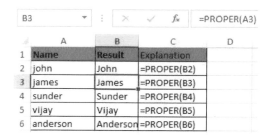

	A	B	C	D
1	Name	Result	Explanation	
2	john	John	=PROPER(B2)	
3	james	James	=PROPER(B3)	
4	sunder	Sunder	=PROPER(B4)	
5	vijay	Vijay	=PROPER(B5)	
6	anderson	Anderson	=PROPER(B6)	

B3 cell: =PROPER(A3)

10.12. REPLACE

This function **replace text based on location** and returns the altered text.

Syntax:

=REPLACE (old_text, start_num, num_chars, new_text)

Parameter list:

old_text - the text to replace.
start_num - the starting location in the text to search.
num_chars - the number of characters to replace.
new_text - the text to replace old_text with.

Points to note.

Use the REPLACE function when you want to replace text based on its location in a string.
Use FIND or SEARCH to find the location of text to replace it if it's not known in advance.
Use SUBSTITUTE to replace text based on content.

10.13. REPT

This function **repeats a text a given number** of times.

Syntax:

=REPT (text, number_times)

Parameter list:

text - the text to repeat.
number_times - the number of times to repeat text.

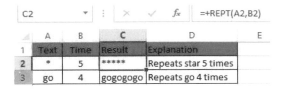

	A	B	C	D	E
1	Text	Time	Result	Explanation	
2	*	5	*****	Repeats star 5 times	
3	go	4	gogogogo	Repeats go 4 times	

C2   fx   =+REPT(A2,B2)

10.14. RIGHT

This function **returns the rightmost characters from a text** as per the number of characters you specify.

Syntax:

=RIGHT (text, [num_chars])

Parameter list:

text - the text from which to extract characters on the right.
num_chars - [optional] the number of characters to extract, starting on the right. Optional, default = 1.

Check the example file exceltovba.com-RIGHT.xls

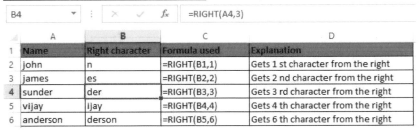

B4   fx   =RIGHT(A4,3)

	A	B	C	D
1	Name	Right character	Formula used	Explanation
2	john	n	=RIGHT(B1,1)	Gets 1 st character from the right
3	james	es	=RIGHT(B2,2)	Gets 2 nd character from the right
4	sunder	der	=RIGHT(B3,3)	Gets 3 rd character from the right
5	vijay	ijay	=RIGHT(B4,4)	Gets 4 th character from the right
6	anderson	derson	=RIGHT(B5,6)	Gets 6 th character from the right

10.15. SEARCH

This function will **return a number representing the location of text** in a string. For example =SEARCH("a","Orange") will return 3 as "a" is in the third position.

Syntax:

=SEARCH (find_text, within_text, [start_num])

Parameter list:

find_text - the text to find.
within_text - the text to search within.
start_num - [optional] starting position in the text to search. Default is 1.

Check the example file exceltovba.com-SEARCH.xls

	A	B	C
1	Name	Result	
2	This is fun	3	=SEARCH("i",A2)
3	This is fun	6	=SEARCH("i",A3,4)
4	How are you doing?	13	=SEARCH("doing",A4)
5	How are you Doing?	13	=SEARCH("doing",A5)
6	How are you Doing?	13	=SEARCH("doi*",A6)
7	How are you Doing?	13	=SEARCH("doi?",A7)

This function is same like FIND function and the main difference is SEARCH allows the use of wildcards and is not case-sensitive.

SEARCH allows the wildcard characters question mark (?) and asterisk (*), in find_text. The ? matches any single character and the * matches any sequence of characters. To find a literal ? or *, use a tilde (~) before the character, i.e. ~* and ~?.

10.16. SUBSTITUTE

This function will **substitute new text into the text string against the old text you specify**. It is like the Find and Replace in the Excel.

Syntax:

=SUBSTITUTE (text, old_text, new_text, [instance])

Parameter list:

text - the text to change.
old_text - the text to replace.
new_text - the text to replace with.
instance – [optional]; if not supplied, all occurrence of old_text are replaced with new_text.

Points to note.

SUBSTITUTE is case-sensitive and does not support wildcards like ? or *.

Check the example file exceltovba.com-SUBSTITUTE.xls

	A	B	C
1	Name	Result	
2	john is john?	vijay is vijay?	=SUBSTITUTE(A2,"john","vijay")
3	john is john?	vijay is john?	=SUBSTITUTE(A3,"john","vijay",1)
4	john is John?	vijay is John?	=SUBSTITUTE(A4,"john","vijay",1)

In the first entry we are substituting the name john with vijay.

In the second entry we are doing the same thing but since the forth parameter we have given as 1 it will substitute only the first occurrence.

Since SUBSTITUTE function is case sensitive it will not substitute the second occurrence of john with vijay in the third entry.

10.17. T

This function **returns the text referred** to by value.

Syntax:

T(value)

Parameter list:

Value - the value you want to test.

If value is or refers to text, T returns value. If value does not refer to text, T returns "" (empty text).

You do not generally need to use the T function in a formula because Microsoft Excel automatically converts values as necessary. This function is provided for compatibility with other spreadsheet programs.

10.18. TEXT

This function **converts a number to text and lets you specify the display formatting by using format strings**. For example, suppose cell A1 contains the number 43.8. To format the number as a dollar amount, you can use the following formula TEXT(A1,"$0.00") and you will get the answer $43.8.

You can also add a text to the preceding formula like this =TEXT(A1,"$0.00") & " per Miles" to get the answer like this $43.8 per Miles.

Syntax:

=TEXT (value, format_text)

Parameter list:

value - The number to convert.
format_text - The number format to use, must appear in double quotation marks. For example "m/d/yyyy" or "#,##0.00"

Complete list of format_text is there in the site **https://support.office.com.**

10.19. TRIM

This function will **remove extra spaces from text from beginning and end**. TRIM removes extra spaces from text, leaving only single spaces between words and no space characters at the start or end of the text.

Syntax:

=TRIM (text)

Parameter list:

text - The text from which to remove extra space.

TRIM is useful when cleaning up text that is been inserted from other Softwares. Also TRIM can be used before using a VLOOKUP function to clear the extra leading and trailing spaces.

10.20. UPPER

This function is used **to change the case of the letter**, in this case to upper case.

Syntax:

= UPPER (text)

Parameter list:

text - the text in a worksheet cell to be changed. The text argument can be

a cell reference like this =UPPER(A1)
a word or words enclosed in quotation marks like this =UPPER("This is Fun")
a formula that outputs text like this =UPPER(CONCATENATE(A4,A5,A6)), will merge all the data In the cell A4, A5 and A6 and change the case to upper.

Check the example file exceltovba.com-UPPER.xls

B3	▾	⋮	✕	✓	*fx*	=UPPER("this is fun")

⊿	A	B	C
1	Name	UPPER	
2	john	JOHN	=UPPER(B2)
3		THIS IS FUN	=UPPER("this is fun")
4	sunder	SUNDERVIJAYANDERSON	=UPPER(CONCATENATE(B4,B5,B6))
5	vijay		
6	anderson		

10.21. VALUE

This function is **used to convert text to a numeric value**. The VALUE function converts text that appears in a recognized format (i.e. a number, date, or time format) into a numeric value.

Syntax:

VALUE(text)

Parameter list:

text - the text enclosed in quotation marks or a reference to a cell containing the text you want to convert.

Normally, Excel automatically converts text to numeric values as needed but in some cases we may get data from other software's that will look like numbers but will be in text format and we will not be able to do any calculation on that, in this case we have to convert the text to numerical value.

If text is not in one of these formats, VALUE returns the #VALUE! error value.

10.22. FIND

This function **get the location of text in a string** and returns a number representing the location.

Syntax:

=FIND (find_text, within_text, [start_num])

Parameter list:

find_text - the text to find.
within_text - the text to search within.
start_num - [optional] the starting position in the text to search, defaults to 1.

Check the example file exceltovba.com-FIND.xls

	A	B	C
1	Name	Result	
2	This is fun	3	=FIND("i",A2)
3	This is fun	6	=FIND("i",A3,4)
4	How are you doing?	13	=FIND("doing",A4)
5	How are you Doing?	#VALUE!	=FIND("doing",A5)

First formula we are finding where the letter "i" starts.
Second formula we have added the third parameter 4 so FIND will search from fourth letter only and will ignore the "i" which is the third letter.
Third formula we are finding the word "doing" from the sentence How are you doing?
Fourth formula again we are searching the word doing since FIND is case sensitive we will get the #VALUE error.

Points to note.

FIND will return #VALUE if find_text is not found in within_text .
FIND is case-sensitive and does not support wildcards.

Conclusion

Hope you have learned new things from my book Excel Formulas.

If these lessons have helped you and found it useful please write a review for this book on Amazon, the more reviews the book gets, the easier the others will be able to find it. I take reviews seriously and always look at them personally and if I think your review is useful, I will mark it as "Helpful".

Once again thanking you for reading this book.

Example file can be downloaded from **ExceltoVBA.com**

Password is **excelformulas@2016**

About the Author

Hi, my name is Vijay Kumar and I 'am crazy about learning as well as teaching Excel. This book is a compilation of the knowledge I have acquired by teaching as well learning Excel from the past few years.

My Other Books.

Excel Shortcuts: 130 Shortcuts that will change your life forever

This book covers various shortcuts from Basic to Advance level in Formatting, Data editing, Selection, Navigation and other useful shortcuts with examples.

These are some of the benefits of learning Shortcuts.

- Increase your productivity by speeder execution of tasks.
- Will increase the accuracy of the work you are doing.
- Help to get Raises and Promotion.
- To impress your Boss and Colleagues.
- It is fun to use the shortcuts.

You can download the book from this link.

http://www.amazon.com/Excel-Shortcuts-that-change-forever-ebook/dp/B01497NDNK/ref=sr_1_2?ie=UTF8&qid=1459075093&sr=8-2&keywords=excel+shortcuts

CPSIA information can be obtained at www.ICGtesting.com
Printed in the USA
LVIW01n0155210318
570508LV00008BA/73

9 781533 061652